DAY BY DAY

Steps to a New Life

by

Dolores E. Shambaugh

and

Herbert B. Puryear, Ph.D.

Based on the Edgar Cayce Readings

A.R.E.® PRESS • VIRGINIA BEACH • VIRGINIA

Use the days, rather than being used by the days.
Edgar Cayce reading number 440-11

THE PURPOSE OF THIS BOOK

is to help you *discover* and *do* the things you want to do so that you may become the best that you can be.

You are aware of the changes you would like to make in your life. But when you think of *all* of them you become overwhelmed. You know the habits you want to eliminate and the ones you want to develop.

You intend to eliminate a habit you know is not good, yet weeks or months pass and you continue in the same pattern. It's discouraging. Then you know why Paul said, "The good that I would I do not: but the evil which I would not, that I do." (Rom. 7:19)

There *is,* however, a way to succeed. If you take these changes *a step at a time,* then each change can gradually become part of your life style. This can be done in a natural way and not be overwhelming.

The Edgar Cayce readings can help you. Day by day, one step at a time, this book—and your desire—will lead you to a better, a more successful life.

How the Readings Can Help You____

The Edgar Cayce readings present the most exciting and the most challenging invitation to a better life. They present the *promise* of a better life.

From these readings you learn again that God is not willing that any soul should perish, that it is the destiny of all children of God to return to oneness with Him. There is the assurance that there is only one force at work in the universe and in your life. That force is not neutral but rather of its very nature it is good and it is love. You are assured that in your soul development there is always progress. Within your own personal life you are assured that there is no condition—physical, mental, emotional or spiritual—that should be remaining unhealed. Any disorder can be completely corrected if appropriate steps are taken consistently and persistently—and with the holistic view of healing.

These readings give you the *information* you need. Every phase of life, physically, mentally, spiritually, socially, and financially is touched upon in a spirit of helpfulness. There is information on how to work with your attitudes and emotions and how to grow in spiritual attunement. The readings' emphasis on application encourages you to take constructive steps in every aspect of your life. The information is sound and practical.

Further, these readings indicate the *qualities of character* you need for change to take place. First and of central importance is will and choice. As you *choose,* as you *decide,* you are given the energy and determination to change. Consistency, persistency and patience are qualities of the soul that *must* one day be manifested. As you begin to apply them in your daily life, there is nothing you cannot accomplish through the living Spirit.

What Is the Key to Success?_____

The readings maintain that the setting of a spiritual ideal is the key to reorienting the motivational thrust of the soul and thereby guaranteeing true success in every life situation. An ideal is not a goal. It is a motivational *standard* by which to *evaluate* your goals and your reasons for pursuing those goals. The goal is *what;* the ideal is *why!*

A spiritual ideal describes the spirit in which you grow. It is a living and dynamic standard by which you quicken and measure your daily motivations. It awakens a high sense of purpose, thus opening the motivational centers through which spiritual energy may flow into your own body and into your relationships with others.

The word which you set as your spiritual ideal should be a word which, when dwelt upon by the *mind*—not the intellect but the imaginative forces of the mind—elicits a response in your body physically, mentally and spiritually. Properly used, such a word inspires the flow of the life forces in and through your being.

When there is a decision to be made or a relationship to consider, dwelling upon the ideal brings the highest motivation to making that decision or dealing with that relationship. When there is difficulty to be met, dwelling upon the ideal enhances your ability to respond to that situation so that its ultimate impact upon everyone is constructive. When there is discouragement, dwelling upon the ideal enhances a deeper sense of the meaningfulness of life and the ever-present power and concern of a loving Father. In each of these situations, using the spiritual ideal guarantees a successful outcome.

At this moment, the step which you are being invited to take may seem unclear, remote or impractical. Yet it is of the utmost importance. It will allow the fullness of your being to respond to this invitation from the universal forces: ". . .the most important experience of this or any individual entity is to first know what *is* the ideal—spiritually." (357-13)

• On the facing page, you see three columns labeled "Spiritual," "Mental," and "Physical." In the first column, record the word or phrase that best describes your *spiritual* ideal. Use pencil, since you'll find you will rethink and refine your words until they most truly reflect your ideal. "Study these. Cross them out, add to them or change. . .the wording as the entity grows." (4041-1) You may at this time want to take a few moments to reflect or meditate, keeping in mind:

"What is thy spiritual concept of the ideal, whether it be Jesus, Buddha, mind, material, God or whatever is the word which indicates to self the ideals spiritual." 5091-3

• After you have written your spiritual ideal, list your areas of concern under "Mental," such as self, home, friends, neighbors, family, job, finances, Study Group, etc. Leave a space between each. Then with respect to *each* of these, record your mental ideal:

"Write the ideal mental *attitude, as may arise from concepts of the spiritual,* relationship to self, to home, to friends, to neighbors, to thy enemies, to things, to conditions." 5091-3

• Next, under "Physical," list the same areas of concern as under "Mental," also leaving a space between each. In that space enter an *ideal course of action* based on the mental and spiritual ideals:

"Not of conditions, but what has brought, *what does bring into manifestation the spiritual and mental ideals."* [authors' italics]5091-3

If under "Physical" you have described an *action,* it's important to follow through. Acting on your ideal makes it a part of you.

In the following example, consider a person who has set "love" as his spiritual ideal. When he comes to the mental ideal, he considers self, home, friends and work. With respect to friends, he asks himself, What ideal mental attitude should arise toward my friends from my spiritual ideal? Then he may have a sense that to be more loving of them, he must have an *attitude* (mental) of forgiveness of himself and others, for he had treated someone unkindly and hadn't seen him since then. He enters "forgive self and others" as an ideal mental attitude. Then under "Physical," he considers ". . .what has brought,

Ideals Worksheet _____

...the most important experience of this or any individual entity is to first know what *is* the ideal—spiritually.   357-13

SPIRITUAL	MENTAL	PHYSICAL

what does bring into manifestation the spiritual and mental ideals. . ."
Now he may say, "To manifest an ideal of forgiveness toward myself, I intend to reestablish our friendship which I have neglected because of unkind words I said." *As he writes the letter to reestablish the relationship,* he *brings into manifestation* (physical ideal) the attitude of forgiveness (mental ideal) which grew out of the motive of love (spiritual ideal).

SPIRITUAL	MENTAL	PHYSICAL
Love	*Self —* *Home —* *Friends —* *forgive self* *and others* *Work —*	*Friends —* *write to* *Richard*

The Edgar Cayce readings see this step for each individual as being of the utmost importance. If you can bring yourself to take this step, to establish a spiritual ideal, you have made a major contribution to the solution of your own problems, for this is a procedure that can be applied to the little things and the big things in life.

Every several weeks, you'll find an Ideals Worksheet in this book. Use it to remind yourself how easy it can be to manifest your spiritual ideal, if you simply take the time for it. . .

" . . . know the ideals . . . Alter them from period to period of real study and meditation. Budget time for physical, mental and material recreation. Let all of these be based on the spiritual outlook . . . "

270-48

Where to Begin

Many people seeking change in their lives were told in the Edgar Cayce readings to begin where they were. . .

"Begin where you are! Everyone should, in every condition with which they are faced, at any period of their experience! . . .When there is a start to be made don't step over! Start where you are, that all may be perfectly understood! for it is line upon line, precept upon precept. We grow in grace, in knowledge, in understanding."   349-1

Where are you now? How do you spend your time each day? Most people are notoriously inaccurate in their estimate of how they spend their time. For example, you may feel that you meditate nearly every day of the week. However, if you keep a record you may find that you are actually averaging only two or three times per week. You may believe your daily schedule cannot contain another activity. Your work, responsibilities of home, commitments to church, a Study Group and some recreation take all the time you have. Yet by keeping track of your activities you will discover you have choices you did not know you had about how you use your time. And you will more surely develop the persistency and consistency that bring new and better habits of thinking, spending and living into your life style.

Many people were told in the readings that they should budget their *time,* not their money. Why is this so? It is simply this: How you use your *time* reflects how you invest your *energies* (and subsequently your financial resources).

The readings emphasize that nothing is asked of any soul but to do what you know to do today. As you apply what you know day by day, the next step is given.

How to Use This Book_____

A whole new year is before you as you begin! You can "begin where you are" without waiting for New Year's to make resolutions. You have sets of planning pages for each week ahead of you. The open calendar format allows you to start your year now by writing the current date at the top of the page for each week.

As you look at the many features of your book, it is appropriate to remind yourself that you are going to proceed day by day, "here a little, there a little," so you do not become overwhelmed. Do keep this in mind.

• One activity that can be most helpful to you is a regular period of **meditation.** Refer to the discussion of meditation on pages 132-133 to review the purpose of meditation, preparation for meditation and the proper techniques for the practice of meditation.

• **Affirmations** from *A Search for God,* Book I, have been selected for each week of the year. You will find each affirmation repeated for a period of four weeks so they may be used in your daily meditation in a twenty-eight-day cycle. Affirmations from *A Search for God,* Book II, are included at the end of this book.

• On each week's planning pages are **Awakeners**—two or three selections from the Edgar Cayce readings (identified by case number). Their purpose is to instruct, remind and quicken you in your attitude toward doing what you need to do each week. As you read and re-read them through the week, you will find both inspiration and practical suggestions.

• Your book can also help you begin and continue with a regular Bible reading program. The readings frequently recommended the Bible as a source of support. When asked which version of the Bible gave the true meaning of both Testaments, the answer was: "The nearest true version for the entity, is that ye apply of whatever version ye read, in your life." (2072-14) Another reading offered this advice:

"Read the Book, if you would get educated. If you would be refined, live it! If you would be beautiful, practice it in thy daily life." (3647-1)

A **Bible Reading Guide** is provided for either of two approaches you may wish to take. If your goal is to read the entire Bible through by the end of the year, you will use the first guide. If you decide to read through just the New Testament this year, then follow the second guide. As you finish your reading each day, check it off so you have a record of your daily progress.

• Space is provided on each weekly page for your **Prayer List.** Prayers for others are a great opportunity and a responsibility. The readings say that many a city, many a nation has been saved from destruction by the prayers of a few who lived the way they prayed.

• Each week you will want to make some specific choices of things to eliminate and others to add. Here is where you begin to tackle the long list of things you feel you should be doing and frequently are not. Space is provided for listing up to a dozen daily activities or practices. The purpose of this weekly list is not to include everything you want to do every day but rather to help you choose only a few changes at a time.

To work with your **Daily Dozen** each week, select several things you've been wanting to do. Remember to challenge yourself, but not overwhelm yourself! Don't select twelve major changes simultaneously.

Also remember it is often easier to make a big change if smaller intermediate steps are taken. For example, you may be planning to increase your daily water intake from your present one or two glasses per day to the six to eight recommended by the readings. The first week you work with this activity, items one and two on your daily dozen list would be "a glass of water upon arising" and "a glass of water upon retiring." You might need to keep these on your list for a couple of weeks before you have it established as a regular pattern. Once you've gotten it established you would no longer write it on your list, but would instead write "drink glass of water before each meal." Soon you would find you were regularly drinking five glasses of water each day. Maintaining that activity, you would then incorporate the additional glasses into your routine in the same fashion and you would arrive at your goal.

Some items will go onto your daily list even though they will happen but once in your week. For example, you may decide to begin attending church or to use a castor oil pack. Your attendance at church might occur just once in your week and the castor oil pack might be three times in the week. Both would be included in your daily dozen list and you would check them off as they were done. Thus your Daily Dozen at the end of a week might look like this:

MY DAILY DOZEN

DATE

		8/16 Sunday	8/17 Monday	8/18 Tuesday	8/19 Wednesday	8/20 Thursday	8/21 Friday	8/22 Saturday
1	Glass of water - arising	✓	✓	✓	✓	✓	✓	✓
2	Glass of water - retiring	✓	✓	✓	✓	✓	✓	✓
3	Head & neck exercises - A.M.	✓	✓	✓	✓	✓	✓	✓
4	Meditation period	✓	✓	✓	✓	✓	✓	✓
5	Read my Bible	✓	✓	✓	✓	✓	✓	✓
6	Prayer for others	✓	✓	✓	✓	✓	✓	✓
7	Attend Church	✓						
8	Castor oil packs			✓	✓	✓		
9	Eliminate carbonated drinks	✓	✓	✓	✓	✓		✓
10	7½ - 8 hours sleep	✓	✓	✓	✓	✓	✓	
11	Salad for lunch	✓	✓	✓	✓	✓	✓	✓
12	A morning walk	✓	✓	✓	✓	✓	✓	✓

Everything you set out to do this sample week was done—except you drank a Coke at work on Friday and your house guests stayed late Saturday night.

You will find suggestions for Daily Dozen activities on page 136 which will help you get started. But *you know* the things you want to be doing—the list is just a guide.

• The way in which you may truly change your life is in the exercise of free will, God's gift to the soul. The basic spiritual problem is the pride of self-will. The basic solution is the humility of "Not my will, but Thine." Consider what a marvelous and glorious thing it would be if at the end of this year you could say you had made specific decisions based on your own inner guidance through meditation and in accord with a high spiritual Ideal! You will find the Edgar Cayce **decision-making procedure** on pages 134-135. Keep a record of these decisions in the space provided each week.

• You will find **note pages** at regular intervals throughout your book. You can record personal advances as seen in your dreams, special insights, or encouraging experiences. Remember, the very nature of life itself is growth and transformation.

• You may find that you need daily **exercises** beginning with gentle exercise, gradually increasing it. If you have not been exercising regularly, you would not want to attempt it all at once. Rather you would choose one exercise that you know you would work with every day before adding others. One man was told, "Have a period for recreation, physically. Don't do this one day, or one day a week. If [you are] not capable of having more than a five-minute walk *every* day, do that! That is better than an hour of strenuous exercise once a month, or even once in a week!" (257-217)

The readings frequently stated that walking was the best exercise for everyone. However, other specific ones were recommended to stimulate the circulation and to maintain flexibility. The exercises illustrated on pages 137-140 are designed to benefit all the major systems of the body.

---

*If you want to know where to get or how to use some of the remedies and suggestions in this book, write to A.R.E. Individual Services Dept., P.O. Box 595, Virginia Beach, VA 23451, for information or a list of suppliers.

- Another feature of your book is the **diet review** sheet on page 141. This guide will enable you to have a handy chart for dietary considerations of things to include and exclude as you work with changes in your eating habits.

- After you have worked with your weekly planning pages for some time, you may discover you want to plan some *series* of activities. These might include spinal adjustments, castor oil packs, weekly massage, facial massage, colonics, epsom salts baths, an Atomidine or Radio-Active Appliance series; for remember:

". . .at least one week out of each month should be spent in beautifying, preserving, rectifying the body—if the body would keep young, in mind, in body, in purpose."   3420-1

You will find your regular monthly calendar an aid. Use your calendar to design your program. Perhaps it would look something like this:

JUNE

SUNDAY	MONDAY	TUESDAY	WEDNESDAY	THURSDAY	FRIDAY	SATURDAY
Radio-Active appliance	1	2	3	4	5 *massage & spinal adjustment*	6
7	8	9	10	11	12	13
14 *Radio-active appliance*	15	16	17	18	19 *← Castor*	20 *oil pack*
21 *on abdomen ——→*	22	23	24	25	26	27
28 *Radio-active appliance*	29	30				

Having planned your month, you would then transfer these activities to your daily dozen list for the appropriate weeks, then do what you know to do one day at a time.

There is a far greater promise of a better life ahead for you than you may ever imagine. You may be assured of a brighter dawn and a brighter day tomorrow. Day by day, you may *the sooner* bring the dawn of that new and better day into your own life and into the lives of those with whom you come in contact. A better you makes a better world.

Week 1 beginning_____

AFFIRMATION

Our Father which art in *heaven,* Hallowed be thy *name.* Thy kingdom come. Thy *will* be done in earth, as it is in heaven. Give us this day our daily *bread.* And forgive us our *debts,* as we forgive our debtors.

And lead us not into *temptation,* but deliver us from *evil:* For thine is the *kingdom,* and the *power,* and the *glory,* for ever.

AWAKENERS

Begin where you are! Everyone should, in every condition with which they are faced, at any period of their experience! Trying to step over, or to jump from one position to another, rather unfits individuals, and makes for those discontentments that come into their lives. Every individual should recognize and understand that Life from its every element or essence is a growth!. . .Start where you are, that all may be perfectly understood! for it is line upon line, precept upon precept. We grow in grace, in knowledge, in understanding.

349-12

For, in all bodies, the less activities there are in physical exercise or manual activity, the greater should be the alkaline-reacting foods taken. *Energies* or activities may burn acids, but those who lead the sedentary life or the non-active life can't go on sweets or too much starches. . .

798-1

BIBLE READING GUIDE

	OLD AND NEW TESTAMENTS	✔	NEW TESTAMENT ONLY
Sunday	Genesis 1-3		Matthew 1
Monday	Genesis 4-6		Matthew 2
Tuesday	Genesis 7-9		Matthew 3
Wednesday	Genesis 10-12		Matthew 4
Thursday	Genesis 13-15		Matthew 5:1-26
Friday	Genesis 16-18		Matthew 5:27-48
Saturday	Genesis 19-21		Matthew 6:1-18

MY PRAYER LIST

MY DAILY DOZEN   **DATE**

	Sunday	Monday	Tuesday	Wednesday	Thursday	Friday	Saturday
1							
2							
3							
4							
5							
6							
7							
8							
9							
10							
11							
12							

DECISIONS

Week 2 beginning _____

AFFIRMATION

Our Father which art in *heaven*, Hallowed be thy *name*. Thy kingdom come. Thy *will* be done in earth, as it is in heaven. Give us this day our daily *bread*. And forgive us our *debts*, as we forgive our debtors.

And lead us not into *temptation*, but deliver us from *evil*: For thine is the *kingdom*, and the *power*, and the *glory*, for ever.

AWAKENERS

Well to drink *always plenty* of water, before meals and after meals—for, as has oft been given, when any food value *enters* the stomach *immediately* the stomach becomes a storehouse, or a medicine chest that may create all the elements necessary for proper digestion within the system. If this *first* is acted upon by aqua pura, the reactions are more near normal.   311-4

. . .ye will find not only more and more that the worthwhileness of life is in being able to see the little things are remembered but that creative forces *grow*, while destructive forces deteriorate.

Then, to be able to remember the sunset, to be able to remember a beautiful conversation, a beautiful deed done where hope and faith were created, to remember the smile of a babe, the blush of a rose, the harmony of a song— a bird's call; *these* are creative. For if they are a part of thyself, they bring you closer and closer to God.

1431-1

BIBLE READING GUIDE

	OLD AND NEW TESTAMENTS	✔	NEW TESTAMENT ONLY
Sunday	Genesis 22-24		Matthew 6:19-34
Monday	Genesis 25-27		Matthew 7
Tuesday	Genesis 28-30		Matthew 8:1-17
Wednesday	Genesis 31-33		Matthew 8:18-34
Thursday	Genesis 34-36		Matthew 9:1-17
Friday	Genesis 37-39		Matthew 9:18-38
Saturday	Genesis 40-42		Matthew 10:1-20

MY PRAYER LIST

MY DAILY DOZEN

DATE

	Sunday	Monday	Tuesday	Wednesday	Thursday	Friday	Saturday
1							
2							
3							
4							
5							
6							
7							
8							
9							
10							
11							
12							

DECISIONS

Week ③ beginning _____

AFFIRMATION

Our Father which art in *heaven,* Hallowed be thy *name.* Thy kingdom come. Thy *will* be done in earth, as it is in heaven. Give us this day our daily *bread.* And forgive us our *debts,* as we forgive our debtors.

And lead us not into *temptation,* but deliver us from *evil:* For thine is the *kingdom,* and the *power,* and the *glory,* for ever.

AWAKENERS

Q. What is the law of love?

A. Giving. . .Giving in action, without the force felt, expressed, manifested, shown, desired or reward for that given.   3744-4

All healing is one, whether in the laying on of hands, by word of mouth, by mechanotherapy, mechanical applications or what not. *God* is the Creative Force that gives life—and not the medicine or the application!   1663-1

Q. Please give some general rules that will help this body to keep in a healthier condition.

A. . . .A general activity for a body in much of a normal condition is to keep the acidity and the alkalinity in a proper balance. The best manner to indicate this is to test the alkalinity or acidity of the body through the salivary glands or through the salivary gland membranes, or by taking the litmus paper in the mouth. This also may be indicated through the urine.   540-11

BIBLE READING GUIDE

	OLD AND NEW TESTAMENTS	✔	NEW TESTAMENT ONLY
Sunday	Genesis 43-45		Matthew 10:21-42
Monday	Genesis 46-48		Matthew 11
Tuesday	Genesis 49-Exodus 1		Matthew 12:1-23
Wednesday	Exodus 2-4		Matthew 12:24-50
Thursday	Exodus 5-7		Matthew 13:1-30
Friday	Exodus 8-10		Matthew 13:31-58
Saturday	Exodus 11-13		Matthew 14:1-21

MY PRAYER LIST

MY DAILY DOZEN   **DATE**

	Sunday	Monday	Tuesday	Wednesday	Thursday	Friday	Saturday
1							
2							
3							
4							
5							
6							
7							
8							
9							
10							
11							
12							

DECISIONS

Week 4 beginning_____

AFFIRMATION

Our Father which art in *heaven,* Hallowed be thy *name.* Thy kingdom come. Thy *will* be done in earth, as it is in heaven. Give us this day our daily *bread.* And forgive us our *debts,* as we forgive our debtors.

And lead us not into *temptation,* but deliver us from *evil:* For thine is the *kingdom,* and the *power,* and the *glory,* for ever.

AWAKENERS

. . .if gelatin will be taken with raw foods rather often (that is, prepare raw vegetables such as carrots often with same, but do not lose the juice from the carrots; grate them, eat them raw), we will help the vision.   5148-1

Q. How may I best develop myself spiritually?

A. Through prayer and meditation. Turn ever to Him for as He has given, practice daily the love of the Christ. For as He gave, "A new commandment I give unto you, that ye love one another." Then manifest that in every way. Let everyone that you meet be happier for having met you, for having spoken to you. This ye can do by spreading joy. This is the manner to unfold, to develop. Then in thy meditation, present thyself as a willing channel, to be as the hands, as the eyes, as the voice of thy Master.

3416-1

It's well that each body, every body, take exercise to counteract the daily routine activity, so as to produce rest.   416-3

BIBLE READING GUIDE

	OLD AND NEW TESTAMENTS	✔	NEW TESTAMENT ONLY
Sunday	Exodus 14-16		Matthew 14:22-36
Monday	Exodus 17-19		Matthew 15:1-20
Tuesday	Exodus 20-22		Matthew 15:21-39
Wednesday	Exodus 23-25		Matthew 16
Thursday	Exodus 26-28		Matthew 17
Friday	Exodus 29-31		Matthew 18:1-20
Saturday	Exodus 32-34		Matthew 18:21-35

MY PRAYER LIST

MY DAILY DOZEN

DATE

	Sunday	Monday	Tuesday	Wednesday	Thursday	Friday	Saturday
1							
2							
3							
4							
5							
6							
7							
8							
9							
10							
11							
12							

DECISIONS

Week 5 beginning_____

AFFIRMATION

Not my will but Thine, O Lord, be done in and through me. Let me ever be a channel of blessings, today, now, to those that I contact, in *every* way. Let my going in, mine coming outs, be in accord with that *Thou* would have me do, and as the call comes, "Here am I, send me—use me!"   262-3

COOPERATION

AWAKENERS

The "why" of the massage should be considered: Inactivity causes many of those portions along the spine from which impulses are received to the various organs to be lax, or taut, or to allow some to receive greater impulse than others. The massage aids the ganglia to receive impulse from nerve forces as it aids circulation through the various portions of the organism.   2456-4

The spirit does not call on anyone to live that it does not already know and understand. In the doing does there come the knowledge, the understanding for the next step. Today, now, is the accepted time!   262-25

We would add those foods that tend to make the eliminations improved; that is, fruits—fresh or raw, as well as cooked; and we would include those that produce better eliminations—figs, raisins, grapes, pears, and the like.   69-4

BIBLE READING GUIDE

	OLD AND NEW TESTAMENTS	✔	NEW TESTAMENT ONLY
Sunday	Exodus 35-37		Matthew 19
Monday	Exodus 38-39		Matthew 20:1-16
Tuesday	Exodus 40		Matthew 20:17-34
Wednesday	Leviticus 1-3		Matthew 21:1-22
Thursday	Leviticus 4-6		Matthew 21:23-46
Friday	Leviticus 7-8		Matthew 22:1-22
Saturday	Leviticus 9-10		Matthew 22:23-46

MY PRAYER LIST

MY DAILY DOZEN

DATE

	Sunday	Monday	Tuesday	Wednesday	Thursday	Friday	Saturday
1							
2							
3							
4							
5							
6							
7							
8							
9							
10							
11							
12							

DECISIONS

Week 6 beginning_____

AFFIRMATION

Not my will but Thine, O Lord, be done in and through me. Let me ever be a channel of blessings, today, now, to those that I contact, in *every* way. Let my going in, mine coming outs, be in accord with that *Thou* would have me do, and as the call comes, "Here am I, send me—use me!"   262-3

AWAKENERS

. . .what we think and what we eat—combined together—*make* what we *are,* physically and mentally.   288-38

Q. Please guide me with information that will enable me to become of greater service to my fellow man.

A. There's none better than we have given, and as may be followed by that which may be brought to the awareness of self through the *practical* application of those meditative forces that come by setting aside a definite time, a period during each day's activity when there will be the purifying of the body, as in accord with that which would make for consecrating of self in all of its efforts, all of its abilities, and entering into the holy of holies within self for that talk with thy God within thyself. These efforts on the part of any soul will bring those things that make for the greater peace and happiness and the abilities to meet those emergencies of every nature that arise within the physical and mental bodies of a living body.   270-33

BIBLE READING GUIDE

	OLD AND NEW TESTAMENTS	✔	NEW TESTAMENT ONLY
Sunday	Leviticus 11-13		Matthew 23:1-22
Monday	Leviticus 14-15		Matthew 23:23-39
Tuesday	Leviticus 16-18		Matthew 24:1-28
Wednesday	Leviticus 19-21		Matthew 24:29-51
Thursday	Leviticus 22-23		Matthew 25:1-30
Friday	Leviticus 24-25		Matthew 25:31-46
Saturday	Leviticus 26-27		Matthew 26:1-25

MY PRAYER LIST

MY DAILY DOZEN

DATE

	Sunday	Monday	Tuesday	Wednesday	Thursday	Friday	Saturday
1							
2							
3							
4							
5							
6							
7							
8							
9							
10							
11							
12							

DECISIONS

Week 7 beginning _____

AFFIRMATION

Not my will but Thine, O Lord, be done in and through me. Let me ever be a channel of blessings, today, now, to those that I contact, in every way. Let my going in, mine coming outs, be in accord with that *Thou* would have me do, and as the call comes, "Here am I, send me—use me!"   262-3

COOPERATION

AWAKENERS

Q. Shall I resume peanut oil rubs?

A. There is nothing better. . .they do supply energies to the body.

And, just as indicated in other suggestions—those who would eat two to three almonds each day need never fear cancer. Those who would take a peanut oil rub each week need never fear arthritis.   1158-31

. . .would that all would learn that He, the Christ Consciousness, is the Giver, the Maker, the Creator of the world and all that be therein! And ye are His. . .He *is,* He *was,* He *ever will be* the expression, the *concrete* expression of *love* in the minds, the hearts, the souls of men. . .He will guide thee, for He hath given His angels charge concerning those that seek to be a channel of blessing to their fellow man. . .696-3

Q. How can I get well-educated, kind and refined associations?

A. Read the Book, if you would get educated. If you would be refined, live it! If you would be beautiful, practice it in thy daily life!   3647-1

BIBLE READING GUIDE

	OLD AND NEW TESTAMENTS	✔	NEW TESTAMENT ONLY
Sunday	Numbers 1-2		Matthew 26:26-50
Monday	Numbers 3-4		Matthew 26:51-75
Tuesday	Numbers 5-6		Matthew 27:1-26
Wednesday	Numbers 7		Matthew 27:27-50
Thursday	Numbers 8-9		Matthew 27:51-66
Friday	Numbers 10-11		Matthew 28
Saturday	Numbers 12-13		Mark 1:1-22

MY PRAYER LIST

MY DAILY DOZEN

DATE

	Sunday	Monday	Tuesday	Wednesday	Thursday	Friday	Saturday
1							
2							
3							
4							
5							
6							
7							
8							
9							
10							
11							
12							

DECISIONS

Week 8 beginning _____

AFFIRMATION

Not my will but Thine, O Lord, be done in and through me. Let me ever be a channel of blessings, today, now, to those that I contact, in every way. Let my going in, mine coming outs, be in accord with that *Thou* would have me do, and as the call comes, "Here am I, send me—use me!"   262-3

COOPERATION

AWAKENERS

First we would begin with the use of hot castor oil packs for about an hour each day for at least three days a week. These would be applied especially across the abdomen in the caecum or in the right area of the body.

Following each three-day period of using the packs, we would take pure olive oil internally; not too great a quantity in the beginning, but as much as the body may assimilate.   2451-1

Remember that a good laugh, an arousing even to what might in some be called hilariousness, is good for the body, physically, mentally, and gives the opportunity for greater mental and spiritual awakening.   2647-1

For each soul should gain that understanding that whatever may be the experience, if there is not resentment, if there is not contention, if there is not the giving of offense, it is for then that soul's own understanding, and will build within the consciousness of the soul itself that which may bring the greater understanding of the spiritual in the physical body.   1242-6

BIBLE READING GUIDE

	OLD AND NEW TESTAMENTS	✔	NEW TESTAMENT ONLY
Sunday	Numbers 14-15		Mark 1:23-45
Monday	Numbers 16-18		Mark 2
Tuesday	Numbers 19-20		Mark 3:1-19
Wednesday	Numbers 21-22		Mark 3:20-35
Thursday	Numbers 23-25		Mark 4:1-20
Friday	Numbers 26-27		Mark 4:21-41
Saturday	Numbers 28-29		Mark 5:1-20

MY PRAYER LIST

MY DAILY DOZEN

DATE

	Sunday	Monday	Tuesday	Wednesday	Thursday	Friday	Saturday
1							
2							
3							
4							
5							
6							
7							
8							
9							
10							
11							
12							

DECISIONS

Notes

Notes

Week 9 beginning _____

AFFIRMATION

Father, as we seek to see and know Thy face, may we each—as individuals, and as a group—come to know ourselves, even as we are known, that we—as lights in Thee—may give the better concept of Thy spirit in this world.   262-5

KNOW THYSELF

AWAKENERS

Q. How can I build up my interest so that I will want to do physical activity?

A. Do it! Only by the application of self. Forcing self to do. Budget the time. Give this much to recreation physically and mentally, give that much to actual service, give so much to actual aid in this or that individual association with an individual or a group or a whole activity with the church, of its own relationships with self and all. Give so much time to each. This will build, *build* that which is constructive.   1089-6

For He has not willed that any soul should perish, but has with every temptation, every trial, prepared a way of escape.

And they that are His, He will not allow to be tempted beyond that they are able to bear.   3292-1

BIBLE READING GUIDE

	OLD AND NEW TESTAMENTS	✔	NEW TESTAMENT ONLY
Sunday	Numbers 30-31		Mark 5:21-43
Monday	Numbers 32-33		Mark 6:1-29
Tuesday	Numbers 34-35		Mark 6:30-56
Wednesday	Numbers 36		Mark 7:1-13
Thursday	Deuteronomy 1-2		Mark 7:14-37
Friday	Deuteronomy 3-4		Mark 8:1-21
Saturday	Deuteronomy 5-7		Mark 8:22-38

MY PRAYER LIST

MY DAILY DOZEN

DATE

	Sunday	Monday	Tuesday	Wednesday	Thursday	Friday	Saturday
1							
2							
3							
4							
5							
6							
7							
8							
9							
10							
11							
12							

DECISIONS

Week 10 beginning _____

AFFIRMATION

Father, as we seek to see and know Thy face, may we each—as individuals, and as a group—come to know ourselves, even as we are known, that we—as lights in Thee—may give the better concept of Thy spirit in this world.　　262-5

KNOW THYSELF

AWAKENERS

Q. Atomidine?*

A. This we would only take as an addition occasionally for the activity or cleansing of the glandular system. When taken, take every day for five days, then leave off. If it's left off for a month or six weeks, the next time it is taken take it every day for five days, then leave off. Small quantity, of course, as we have indicated.　　1158-21

...and the messages found in the 14th, 15th, 16th and 17th chapters of St. John... As you read, apply the messages not just to anyone but to SELF—as though He, the Lord, were speaking alone with thee! Read only about five to ten verses each day. Then apply that given in those verses for a day! Then read five to ten more—apply that. You will find a regeneration.　　2067-6

In budgeting thy time, do not set thyself to activities spasmodically—for body improvement in *any* respect, or periodically; but rather systematically.　　1206-13

*For information and list of suppliers, write to A.R.E. Individual Services.

BIBLE READING GUIDE

	OLD AND NEW TESTAMENTS	✔	NEW TESTAMENT ONLY
Sunday	Deuteronomy 8-10		Mark 9:1-29
Monday	Deuteronomy 11-13		Mark 9:30-50
Tuesday	Deuteronomy 14-16		Mark 10:1-31
Wednesday	Deuteronomy 17-20		Mark 10:32-52
Thursday	Deuteronomy 21-23		Mark 11:1-18
Friday	Deuteronomy 24-27		Mark 11:19-33
Saturday	Deuteronomy 28		Mark 12:1-27

MY PRAYER LIST

MY DAILY DOZEN

DATE

	Sunday	Monday	Tuesday	Wednesday	Thursday	Friday	Saturday
1							
2							
3							
4							
5							
6							
7							
8							
9							
10							
11							
12							

DECISIONS

Week 11 beginning___

AFFIRMATION

Father, as we seek to see and know Thy face, may we each—as individuals, and as a group—come to know ourselves, even as we are known, that we—as lights in Thee—may give the better concept of Thy spirit in this world.   262-5

AWAKENERS

Do not have large quantities of any fruits, vegetables, meats, that are not grown in or come to the area where the body is at the time it partakes of such foods. This will be found to be a good rule to be followed by all. This prepares the system to acclimate itself to any given territory.   3542-1

For this entity should comprehend and *know* and *never* forget, that life and its experiences are only what one puts into same! And unless the activities, the thoughts are *continuously* constructive, and the experience well-balanced, the entity *cannot, will* not fulfill the purpose for which it came into the present experience.   1537-1

As it is necessary for recreation and rest for the physical, so it is necessary that there be recreation and rest for the mental.   3691-1

BIBLE READING GUIDE

	OLD AND NEW TESTAMENTS	✔	NEW TESTAMENT ONLY
Sunday	Deuteronomy 29-31		Mark 12:28-44
Monday	Deuteronomy 32-34		Mark 13:1-20
Tuesday	Joshua 1-3		Mark 13:21-37
Wednesday	Joshua 4-6		Mark 14:1-26
Thursday	Joshua 7-8		Mark 14:27-53
Friday	Joshua 9-10		Mark 14:54-72
Saturday	Joshua 11-13		Mark 15:1-25

MY PRAYER LIST

MY DAILY DOZEN

DATE

	Sunday	Monday	Tuesday	Wednesday	Thursday	Friday	Saturday
1							
2							
3							
4							
5							
6							
7							
8							
9							
10							
11							
12							

DECISIONS

Week 12 beginning_____

AFFIRMATION

Father, as we seek to see and know Thy face, may we each—as individuals, and as a group—come to know ourselves, even as we are known, that we—as lights in Thee—may give the better concept of Thy spirit in this world.   262-5

AWAKENERS

Q. Advise regarding body's health, as to best manner to keep physically fit.
A. Keep well! Keep in that of rather the position of not having to be cured *of,* but rather that as *preventative* activities—physical and mental. The body very good in this respect. . .for the body is not prone to overtax self mentally—which is very good. Were most people to act in the same way they would all be better off!   1565-2

So in thy dealings with others, with thy problems with others, in thy daily associations, in thy home, in thy activities—remember to evaluate *every* phase of an experience and to stress the beautiful, minimize the faults. For, this is sowing the seed of beauty in the spirit of truth; and that, too, will blossom in thy life and in thy dealings with others.   2448-2

BIBLE READING GUIDE

	OLD AND NEW TESTAMENTS	✔	NEW TESTAMENT ONLY
Sunday	Joshua 14-16		Mark 15:26-47
Monday	Joshua 17-19		Mark 16
Tuesday	Joshua 20-21		Luke 1:1-20
Wednesday	Joshua 22-24		Luke 1:21-38
Thursday	Judges 1-2		Luke 1:39-56
Friday	Judges 3-5		Luke 1:57-80
Saturday	Judges 6-7		Luke 2:1-24

MY PRAYER LIST

MY DAILY DOZEN

DATE

	Sunday	Monday	Tuesday	Wednesday	Thursday	Friday	Saturday
1							
2							
3							
4							
5							
6							
7							
8							
9							
10							
11							
12							

DECISIONS

Notes

Ideals Worksheet_____

...the most important experience of this or any individual entity is to first know what *is* the ideal—spiritually.   357-13

SPIRITUAL	MENTAL	PHYSICAL

Week 13 beginning_____

AFFIRMATION

God be merciful to me! Help Thou my unbelief! Let me *see* in Him that Thou would have me see in my fellow man! Let me see in my brother that I see in Him whom I worship!   262-11

WHAT IS MY IDEAL?

AWAKENERS

Keep the eliminations in the system (that is, through the intestinal tract) acting normally and properly, even though enemas and cleansing of the colon is resorted to—which is well for anyone to do. . .   5712-1

Q. Please expand on how we can learn.
A. So oft has this been given, and though it may be repeated again and again, there is only one way. *Use that thou hast in hand day by day,* for knowledge and understanding come with the application and the *experience* of self in *doing* that which is *known* to be in accord with His will. Example after example may be given in the experience of *any* individual. As they *apply* that known, knowing in whom they *have* believed, *with* the comparisons of the ideal as the standard, as the gauge and judge, they come to the knowledge of the forces that are manifest from experience to experience, from day to day.   281-8

BIBLE READING GUIDE

	OLD AND NEW TESTAMENTS	✔	NEW TESTAMENT ONLY
Sunday	Judges 8-9		Luke 2:25-52
Monday	Judges 10-11		Luke 3
Tuesday	Judges 12-14		Luke 4:1-30
Wednesday	Judges 15-17		Luke 4:31-44
Thursday	Judges 18-19		Luke 5:1-16
Friday	Judges 20-21		Luke 5:17-39
Saturday	Ruth 1-4		Luke 6:1-26

MY PRAYER LIST

MY DAILY DOZEN

DATE

	Sunday	Monday	Tuesday	Wednesday	Thursday	Friday	Saturday
1							
2							
3							
4							
5							
6							
7							
8							
9							
10							
11							
12							

DECISIONS

Week 14 beginning_____

AFFIRMATION

God be merciful to me! Help Thou my unbelief! Let me *see* in Him that Thou would have me see in my fellow man! Let me see in my brother that I see in Him whom I worship! 262-11

AWAKENERS:

During the periods especially when there is the use of the Radio-Active Appliance,* we would use these periods as the periods for meditation; that there may be brought a better coordination between the nervous systems of the body, at such periods opening—through suggestions to self in meditation or prayer—the centers that coordinate the spiritual forces and influences with the mental and physical body; using as a guide (though in thine own words) such as this:

Father, God! In Thy Love, in Thy mercy, be Thou the guide: that my body, my mind, my self, may fulfill Thy purpose in this material plane at this time. 2164-1

For he that contributes only to his own welfare soon finds little to work for. He that contributes only to the welfare of others soon finds too much of others and has lost the appreciation of self, or of its ideals. 3478-2

*For information and list of suppliers, write to A.R.E. Individual Services

BIBLE READING GUIDE

	OLD AND NEW TESTAMENTS	✔	NEW TESTAMENT ONLY
Sunday	I Samuel 1-3		Luke 6:27-49
Monday	I Samuel 4-7		Luke 7: 1-30
Tuesday	I Samuel 8-11		Luke 7:31-50
Wednesday	I Samuel 12-14:23		Luke 8:1-25
Thursday	I Samuel 14:24-16		Luke 8:26-56
Friday	I Samuel 17-18		Luke 9:1-17
Saturday	I Samuel 19-21		Luke 9:18-36

MY PRAYER LIST

MY DAILY DOZEN

DATE

	Sunday	Monday	Tuesday	Wednesday	Thursday	Friday	Saturday
1							
2							
3							
4							
5							
6							
7							
8							
9							
10							
11							
12							

DECISIONS

Week 15 beginning_____

AFFIRMATION

God be merciful to me! Help Thou my unbelief! Let me *see* in Him that Thou would have me see in my fellow man! Let me see in my brother that I see in Him whom I worship!   262-11

AWAKENERS

. . .the blood supply is added to three times each day if meals are taken, else we would never recuperate or change a whole body every seven years; it is a *constant* growth. No condition of a physical nature should be *remaining* unless it has been hamstrung by operative forces or strictures or tissue that may not be absorbed; and even this may be changed if it is taken patiently and persistently—in *any* body!   133-4

Mind. . .is ever the Builder, and. . .the key should be making, compelling, inducing, having the Mind one with that which is the Ideal.   262-84

Turn about, and pray a little oftener. Do this several weeks, yes—let a whole moon pass, or a period of a moon—28 days—and never fail to pray at two o'clock in the morning. Rise and pray—facing east! Ye will be surprised at how much peace and harmony will come into thy soul.   3509-1

BIBLE READING GUIDE

	OLD AND NEW TESTAMENTS	✔	NEW TESTAMENT ONLY
Sunday	I Samuel 22-24		Luke 9:37-62
Monday	I Samuel 25-27		Luke 10:1-24
Tuesday	I Samuel 28-31		Luke 10:25-42
Wednesday	II Samuel 1-2		Luke 11:1-28
Thursday	II Samuel 3-5		Luke 11:29-54
Friday	II Samuel 6-9		Luke 12:1-31
Saturday	II Samuel 10-12		Luke 12:32-59

MY PRAYER LIST

48

MY DAILY DOZEN   **DATE**

	Sunday	Monday	Tuesday	Wednesday	Thursday	Friday	Saturday
1							
2							
3							
4							
5							
6							
7							
8							
9							
10							
11							
12							

DECISIONS

Week 16 beginning_____

AFFIRMATION

God be merciful to me! Help Thou my unbelief! Let me *see* in Him that Thou would have me see in my fellow man! Let me see in my brother that I see in Him whom I worship!   262-11

WHAT IS MY IDEAL?

AWAKENERS

. . . there must be a budgeting of time. Take time to recuperate, physically, mentally and spiritually; not merely by outward saying. For, if these are not done for this entity, as well as any other entity, the entity becomes either self-centered or lopsided in his estimates or values in a material or life experience. Take time to be holy. Take time to pray. Take time to rest, to study, to be an associate with individuals, to have the proper associates. Take time to work, and work like the devil when you are working at it! But, as ye profess, keep *holy* in the service of God and man.   257-254

Q. For what purpose did I come to the earth plane at this time?
A. As *everyone*; for further development of the I AM towards a cooperative, coordinating activity with the Creative Forces that manifest themselves through the activity of an individual in materiality or the earth. That would be for anyone.
649-2

BIBLE READING GUIDE

	OLD AND NEW TESTAMENTS	✔	NEW TESTAMENT ONLY
Sunday	II Samuel 13-14		Luke 13:1-22
Monday	II Samuel 15-16		Luke 13:23-35
Tuesday	II Samuel 17-18		Luke 14:1-24
Wednesday	II Samuel 19-20		Luke 14:25-35
Thursday	II Samuel 21-22		Luke 15:1-10
Friday	II Samuel 23-24		Luke 15:11-32
Saturday	I Kings 1-2:25		Luke 16

MY PRAYER LIST

MY DAILY DOZEN

DATE

	Sunday	Monday	Tuesday	Wednesday	Thursday	Friday	Saturday
1							
2							
3							
4							
5							
6							
7							
8							
9							
10							
11							
12							

DECISIONS

Notes_____

Notes

Week 17 beginning _____

AFFIRMATION

Create in me a pure heart, O God! Open Thou mine heart to the faith Thou has implanted in all that seek Thy face! Help Thou mine unbelief in my God, in my neighbor, in myself.   262-13

FAITH

AWAKENERS

Q. What is best way to relax my head, when I translate or read a lot?
A. Relax the body fully, just before attempting same, by repose. Then a little head and neck exercise. And after such experiences *again* a thorough relaxing, with plenty of water taken internally, and a little head and neck exercise; and we will find the responses to quick recuperative forces.

...in carrying impressions as from individual to individual in the form of words...one often draws upon one's nervous energy; which becomes, to be sure, by posture, localized in the upper cervical or through the neck, between the shoulders and to the head.

Yet with the...exercises...and with water, these produce as it were a recharging of the battery forces of the bodily functionings.   1554-4

If thou wouldst have shown forth to thee that of brotherly love, then show same to thy friend, thy neighbor, thine enemy, thine stranger, that ye meet day by day. Such will make for growth, for the attraction of the proper relationships in the experiences and affairs of *any* individual.   551-13

BIBLE READING GUIDE

	OLD AND NEW TESTAMENTS	✔	NEW TESTAMENT ONLY
Sunday	I Kings 2:26-4		Luke 17:1-19
Monday	I Kings 5-7		Luke 17:20-37
Tuesday	I Kings 8		Luke 18:1-23
Wednesday	I Kings 9-11		Luke 18:24-43
Thursday	I Kings 12-13		Luke 19:1-27
Friday	I Kings 14-15		Luke 19:28-48
Saturday	I Kings 16-18		Luke 20:1-26

MY PRAYER LIST

MY DAILY DOZEN

DATE

	Sunday	Monday	Tuesday	Wednesday	Thursday	Friday	Saturday
1							
2							
3							
4							
5							
6							
7							
8							
9							
10							
11							
12							

DECISIONS

Week 18 beginning_____

AFFIRMATION

Create in me a pure heart, O God! Open Thou mine heart to the faith Thou has implanted in all that seek Thy face! Help Thou mine unbelief in my God, in my neighbor, in myself.   262-13

FAITH

AWAKENERS

Then the diet: This should be not so rigid as to appear that you can't do this or you can't do that, but rather let the attitudes be—everything that is eaten, as well as every activity—purposeful in conception, constructive in nature. Analyze that! Purposeful in activity, constructive in nature!   1183-2

Q. What charitable work can I do to make me more worthy to my fellow man?
A. It isn't charitable work that's needed! It's yourself that's needed. It is yourself that you need to expend in helping others! Charity doesn't go much farther than the fellow you contact talking about what a big fellow you are in glorifying yourself in an organized work. But serving yourself is quite different—and is that which counts the most.   2981-4

BIBLE READING GUIDE

	OLD AND NEW TESTAMENTS	✔	NEW TESTAMENT ONLY
Sunday	I Kings 19-20		Luke 20:27-47
Monday	I Kings 21-22		Luke 21:1-19
Tuesday	II Kings 1-3		Luke 21:20-38
Wednesday	II Kings 4-5		Luke 22:1-20
Thursday	II Kings 6-8		Luke 22:21-46
Friday	II Kings 9-10		Luke 22:47-71
Saturday	II Kings 11-13		Luke 23:1-25

MY PRAYER LIST

MY DAILY DOZEN

DATE

	Sunday	Monday	Tuesday	Wednesday	Thursday	Friday	Saturday
1							
2							
3							
4							
5							
6							
7							
8							
9							
10							
11							
12							

DECISIONS

Week 19 beginning_____

AFFIRMATION

Create in me a pure heart, O God! Open Thou mine heart to the faith Thou has implanted in all that seek Thy face! Help Thou mine unbelief in my God, in my neighbor, in myself. 262-13

FAITH

AWAKENERS

When once the cold has attacked the body, there are certain measures that should always be taken.

First, as has so often been indicated, *rest!* Do not attempt to go on, but *rest!* For, there is the indication of an exhaustion somewhere, else the body would not have been susceptible. . .

Then, find or determine next where the weakness lies. Is it from lack of eliminations (which causes many ailments)?

Hence quantities of water, as well as an alkalizer, as well as a booster to assimilating forces, are beneficial things towards producing a balance so that the cold and its consequences may be the more readily or easily eliminated or eradicated.

902-1

Not that any soul that seeks for the revelation from the Spirit-God into their own lives would become long-faced nor one that mopes or gropes about; for who should be the happiest people in the earth? They that walk and talk with Life day by day! What is Life? God in expression in the earth! 610-1

BIBLE READING GUIDE

	OLD AND NEW TESTAMENTS	✔	NEW TESTAMENT ONLY
Sunday	II Kings 14-15		Luke 23:26-56
Monday	II Kings 16-17		Luke 24:1-35
Tuesday	II Kings 18-20		Luke 24:36-53
Wednesday	iI Kings 21-23:20		John 1:1-28
Thursday	II Kings 23:21-25		John 1:29-51
Friday	I Chronicles 1-2		John 2
Saturday	I Chronicles 3-5		John 3:1-18

MY PRAYER LIST

MY DAILY DOZEN

DATE

	Sunday	Monday	Tuesday	Wednesday	Thursday	Friday	Saturday
1							
2							
3							
4							
5							
6							
7							
8							
9							
10							
11							
12							

DECISIONS

Week 20 beginning_____

AFFIRMATION

Create in me a pure heart, O God! Open Thou mine heart to the faith Thou has implanted in all that seek Thy face! Help Thou mine unbelief in my God, in my neighbor, in myself.   262-13

FAITH

AWAKENERS

Know that all healing forces must be within, *not* without! The applications from without are to create within a coordinating mental and spiritual force. Set the mind to believe in *something,* and let that be creative. . .   1196-7

As indicated for most people and it is very well here: don't get mad and don't cuss a body out mentally or in voice. This brings more poisons than may be created by even taking foods that aren't good.   470-37

Do not lose faith in *self,* for if faith is lost in self and self's abilities to accomplish, then there is already defeat staring thee in the face! This would be true for every individual. Becoming discouraged only lessens the capacities of individuals to become aware of that consciousness of the divine forces and divine rights that may be sought by each individual, if it is doing that which enables it to look its Savior, its guide, its Lord in the face and say, "I have done my best."   257-131

BIBLE READING GUIDE

	OLD AND NEW TESTAMENTS		NEW TESTAMENT ONLY
Sunday	I Chronicles 6-7		John 3:19-36
Monday	I Chronicles 8-10		John 4:1-30
Tuesday	I Chronicles 11-13		John 4:31-54
Wednesday	I Chronicles 14-16		John 5:1-24
Thursday	I Chronicles 17-20		John 5:25-47
Friday	I Chronicles 21-23		John 6:1-21
Saturday	I Chronicles 24-26		John 6:22-44

MY PRAYER LIST

MY DAILY DOZEN

DATE

	Sunday	Monday	Tuesday	Wednesday	Thursday	Friday	Saturday
1							
2							
3							
4							
5							
6							
7							
8							
9							
10							
11							
12							

DECISIONS

Week 21 beginning _____

AFFIRMATION

Let virtue and understanding be in me, for my defense is in Thee, O Lord, my Redeemer; for Thou hearest the prayer of the upright in heart.   262-17

AWAKENERS

Have a period for recreation, physically. Don't do this one day, or one day a week. If it is not capable of having more than a five-minute walk *every* day, do that! That is better than an hour of strenuous exercise once a month, or even once in a week!
                                                                                                    257-217

. . .according to the true law of spirit, like begets like. Thus as harmony and beauty and grace reign within the consciousness of an entity, it gives that to others—and others wonder what moved them to feel different, when no one spoke, no one even appeared to be anxious. This is the manner in which the spirit of truth operates among the children of men.   3098-2

Remember, the body does gradually renew itself constantly. Do not look upon the conditions which have existed as not being able to be eradicated from the system.
                                                                                                    1548-3

BIBLE READING GUIDE

	OLD AND NEW TESTAMENTS	✔	NEW TESTAMENT ONLY
Sunday	I Chronicles 27-29		John 6:45-71
Monday	II Chronicles 1-3		John 7:1-27
Tuesday	II Chronicles 4-6		John 7:28-52
Wednesday	II Chronicles 7-9		John 8:1-27
Thursday	II Chronicles 10-13		John 8:28-59
Friday	II Chronicles 14-17		John 9:1-23
Saturday	II Chronicles 18-20		John 9:24-41

MY PRAYER LIST

MY DAILY DOZEN

DATE

	Sunday	Monday	Tuesday	Wednesday	Thursday	Friday	Saturday
1							
2							
3							
4							
5							
6							
7							
8							
9							
10							
11							
12							

DECISIONS

Week 22 beginning———————

AFFIRMATION

Let virtue and understanding be in me, for my defense is in Thee, O Lord, my Redeemer; for Thou hearest the prayer of the upright in heart.   262-17

AWAKENERS

Q. What is the best cleanser for teeth?
A. Equal combinations of salt and soda—calcium chloride and bicarbonate of soda, equal parts. Nothing better!   276-7

Q. What passages especially should he read in the Bible?
A. The admonition of Moses, the creation of man in the first three chapters, the admonition of Joshua, the 1st Psalm, the 2nd and 4th Psalm, the 22nd, 23rd and 24th Psalm, the 91st Psalm, the 12th of Romans, the 14th, 15th, 16th, 17th of John, 13th of 2nd Corinthians [I Cor. 13?] and the Book of Revelation.

And in the Revelation study as this: Know, as there is given each emblem, each condition, it is representing or presenting to self a study of thine own body, with *all* of its emotions, all of its faculties. All of its physical centers represent experiences through which thine own mental and spiritual and physical being pass. For it is indeed the revelation of self.   1173-8

BIBLE READING GUIDE

	OLD AND NEW TESTAMENTS	✔	NEW TESTAMENT ONLY
Sunday	II Chronicles 21-24		John 10:1-23
Monday	II Chronicles 25-27		John 10:24-42
Tuesday	II Chronicles 28-30		John 11:1-29
Wednesday	II Chronicles 31-33		John 11:30-57
Thursday	II Chronicles 34-36		John 12:1-26
Friday	Ezra 1-2		John 12:27-50
Saturday	Ezra 3-5		John 13:1-20

MY PRAYER LIST

MY DAILY DOZEN

DATE

	Sunday	Monday	Tuesday	Wednesday	Thursday	Friday	Saturday
1							
2							
3							
4							
5							
6							
7							
8							
9							
10							
11							
12							

DECISIONS

Week 23 beginning _____

AFFIRMATION

Let virtue and understanding be in me, for my defense is in Thee, O Lord, my Redeemer; for Thou hearest the prayer of the upright in heart. 262-17

VIRTUE AND UNDERSTANDING

AWAKENERS

. . .for would the assimilations and eliminations be kept nearer *normal* in the human family, the days might be extended to whatever period as was so desired; for the system is *builded* by the assimilations of that it takes within, and is able to bring resuscitation so long as the eliminations do not hinder. 311-4

All work and no play is as bad as all play with no work. 2597-2

. . .each soul must of itself *find* the answer within self. For indeed the body is the temple of the living God. There He has promised to meet thee; there He does. And as thy body, thy mind, thy soul is attuned to that divine as answers within, so may ye indeed be quickened to know His purpose; and ye may fill that purpose for which ye entered this experience. 69-4

BIBLE READING GUIDE

	OLD AND NEW TESTAMENTS	✔	NEW TESTAMENT ONLY
Sunday	Ezra 6-7		John 13:21-38
Monday	Ezra 8-9		John 14
Tuesday	Ezra 10		John 15
Wednesday	Nehemiah 1-3		John 16
Thursday	Nehemiah 4-6		John 17
Friday	Nehemiah 7-8		John 18:1-18
Saturday	Nehemiah 9-10		John 18:19-40

MY PRAYER LIST

MY DAILY DOZEN

DATE

	Sunday	Monday	Tuesday	Wednesday	Thursday	Friday	Saturday
1							
2							
3							
4							
5							
6							
7							
8							
9							
10							
11							
12							

DECISIONS

Week 24 beginning_____

AFFIRMATION

Let virtue and understanding be in me, for my defense is in Thee, O Lord, my Redeemer; for Thou hearest the prayer of the upright in heart.　　　262-17

AWAKENERS

. . .train self never to bolt the food. Take *time* to assimilate, masticate, so that *assimilation* is well and we will find that with these kept, with an *even* balance between those that produce acid and those that make for the alkaline, if well balanced will digest under most all circumstances.　　　311-4

A good lesson here for everyone to learn who would know the way of the Lord! Be patient, be just, be kind, be long-suffering, show brotherly love—and then don't worry about what's going to happen! but be sure you do these! When you get to the place where you would worry (this is for the entity), stop and pray! For why worry, when you can pray? For God is not mocked, and He remembers thee in thy sincerity in thy purpose.　　　2823-3

. . .in the doing for others there comes the answer to the problems for self; in every direction.　　　2174-3

BIBLE READING GUIDE

	OLD AND NEW TESTAMENTS	✔	NEW TESTAMENT ONLY
Sunday	Nehemiah 11-12		John 19:1-22
Monday	Nehemiah 13		John 19:23-42
Tuesday	Esther 1-3		John 20
Wednesday	Esther 4-7		John 21
Thursday	Esther 8-10		Acts 1
Friday	Job 1-4		Acts 2:1-21
Saturday	Job 5-8		Acts 2:22-47

MY PRAYER LIST

MY DAILY DOZEN

DATE

	Sunday	Monday	Tuesday	Wednesday	Thursday	Friday	Saturday
1							
2							
3							
4							
5							
6							
7							
8							
9							
10							
11							
12							

DECISIONS

Notes

Ideals Worksheet_____

...the most important experience of this or any individual entity is to
first know what *is* the ideal—spiritually.   357-13

SPIRITUAL	MENTAL	PHYSICAL

Week 25 beginning _____

AFFIRMATION

How excellent is Thy name in the earth, O Lord! Would I have fellowship with Thee, I must show brotherly love to my fellow man. Though I come in humbleness and have aught against my brother, my prayer, my meditation, does not rise to Thee. Help Thou my efforts in my approach to Thee.   262-21

FELLOWSHIP

AWAKENERS

At least once a week, after a good, thorough workout of body in exercise—following the bath afterward, massage the back, the face, the body, the limbs with pure peanut oil. Then this will add to the beauty. . .And the oil rubs once a week, ye will never have rheumatism nor those concurrent conditions from stalemate in liver and kidney activities.   1206-13

Unless the entity, unless the body looks upon the experiences day by day as necessary influences and forces, and uses them as a stepping-stone, soon does life become a pessimistic outlook. If each and every disappointment, each and every condition that arises, is used as a stepping-stone for better things and looking for it and expecting it, then there will still be continued the optimism. Or the looking for and expecting of. If an individual doesn't expect great things of God, he has a very poor God, hasn't he?   462-10

BIBLE READING GUIDE

	OLD AND NEW TESTAMENTS	✔	NEW TESTAMENT ONLY
Sunday	Job 9-12		Acts 3
Monday	Job 13-16		Acts 4:1-22
Tuesday	Job 17-20		Acts 4:23-37
Wednesday	Job 21-24		Acts 5:1-21
Thursday	Job 25-29		Acts 5:22-42
Friday	Job 30-33		Acts 6
Saturday	Job 34-37		Acts 7:1-21

MY PRAYER LIST

MY DAILY DOZEN

DATE

	Sunday	Monday	Tuesday	Wednesday	Thursday	Friday	Saturday
1							
2							
3							
4							
5							
6							
7							
8							
9							
10							
11							
12							

DECISIONS

Week 26 beginning _____

AFFIRMATION

How excellent is Thy name in the earth, O Lord! Would I have fellowship with Thee, I must show brotherly love to my fellow man. Though I come in humbleness and have aught against my brother, my prayer, my meditation, does not rise to Thee. Help Thou my efforts in my approach to Thee.   262-21

FELLOWSHIP

AWAKENERS

Q. How can I utilize my evenings and Sundays to best advantage?
A. . . .These have been met in, "Remember the Sabbath to keep it holy." [Ex. 20:8] Then *one* day must be kept in that way that will feed the mental and *spiritual* life of a body. All work and no play will destroy the best of abilities. Yet these have been set in the manner as is outlined in the *spirit* of "Remember to keep the day holy."   349-6

Whether in the mental, the physical or the spiritual, have an ideal; and not be merely idealistic. Be true, be consistent. And oh that all might know that consistency is indeed a jewel in the experiences of any! Never ask of others that ye do not do yourself. Never require of others that ye do not practice in thy own experience.   1610-2

BIBLE READING GUIDE

	OLD AND NEW TESTAMENTS	✔	NEW TESTAMENT ONLY
Sunday	Job 38-40		Acts 7:22-43
Monday	Job 41-42		Acts 7:44-60
Tuesday	Psalms 1-9		Acts 8:1-25
Wednesday	Psalms 10-17		Acts 8:26-40
Thursday	Psalms 18-22		Acts 9:1-21
Friday	Psalms 23-30		Acts 9:22-43
Saturday	Psalms 31-35		Acts 10:1-23

MY PRAYER LIST

MY DAILY DOZEN

DATE

	Sunday	Monday	Tuesday	Wednesday	Thursday	Friday	Saturday
1							
2							
3							
4							
5							
6							
7							
8							
9							
10							
11							
12							

DECISIONS

Week 27 beginning _____

AFFIRMATION

How excellent is Thy name in the earth, O Lord! Would I have fellowship with Thee, I must show brotherly love to my fellow man. Though I come in humbleness and have aught against my brother, my prayer, my meditation, does not rise to Thee. Help Thou my efforts in my approach to Thee.   262-21

FELLOWSHIP

AWAKENERS

Q. How can the body relax?
A. This a *mental* as well as a physical process.
Concentration upon relaxation is the greater or better manner for *any* body to relax. That is, SEE the body *relaxing,* CONSCIOUSLY! Not concentrating so as to draw *in* the influence, but as to let all of the tension, all of the strain, flow OUT of self—and find the body giving—giving—away.   404-6

What need is there for a better body, save to serve thy fellow man the better? For he that is the greatest among you is the servant of all. This is not only referring to those who teach, to those who minister, to those who wait on this, that or the other influence, but to each and every soul—and to every phase of the soul's activity in a material world!   1620-1

BIBLE READING GUIDE

	OLD AND NEW TESTAMENTS	✔	NEW TESTAMENT ONLY
Sunday	Psalms 36-39		Acts 10:24-48
Monday	Psalms 40-45		Acts 11
Tuesday	Psalms 46-51		Acts 12
Wednesday	Psalms 52-59		Acts 13:1-25
Thursday	Psalms 60-66		Acts 13:26-52
Friday	Psalms 67-71		Acts 14
Saturday	Psalms 72-77		Acts 15:1-21

MY PRAYER LIST

MY DAILY DOZEN

DATE

	Sunday	Monday	Tuesday	Wednesday	Thursday	Friday	Saturday
1							
2							
3							
4							
5							
6							
7							
8							
9							
10							
11							
12							

DECISIONS

Week 28 beginning_____

AFFIRMATION

How excellent is Thy name in the earth, O Lord! Would I have fellowship with Thee, I must show brotherly love to my fellow man. Though I come in humbleness and have aught against my brother, my prayer, my meditation, does not rise to Thee. Help Thou my efforts in my approach to Thee. 262-21

FELLOWSHIP

AWAKENERS

Q. Would smoking be detrimental to me or beneficial?
A. This depends very much upon self. In moderation, smoking is not harmful; but to a body that holds such as being out of line with its best mental or spiritual unfoldment, do not smoke. 2981-2

. . .there should be more water taken in the system, in more consistent manner, that the system, especially in the hepatics and kidneys, may function more nominally, thus producing the correct manner for eliminations of drosses. . . 257-11

He hath not willed, He hath not destined that any soul should perish. In patience, in persistency, in consistency of thy manifestations of His love before and to and of thy fellow man, ye become aware that thy soul is a portion of the Creator, that it is the gift of the Father *to thee*. . .
Then, just being kind, just being patient, just showing love for thy follow man; *that* is the manner in which an individual works *at* becoming aware of the consciousness of the Christ Spirit. 272-9

BIBLE READING GUIDE

	OLD AND NEW TESTAMENTS	✔	NEW TESTAMENT ONLY
Sunday	Psalms 78-80		Acts 15:22-41
Monday	Psalms 81-87		Acts 16:1-21
Tuesday	Psalms 88-91		Acts 16:22-40
Wednesday	Psalms 92-100		Acts 17:1-15
Thursday	Psalms 101-105		Acts 17:16-34
Friday	Psalms 106-107		Acts 18
Saturday	Psalms 108-118		Acts 19:1-20

MY PRAYER LIST

MY DAILY DOZEN

DATE

	Sunday	Monday	Tuesday	Wednesday	Thursday	Friday	Saturday
1							
2							
3							
4							
5							
6							
7							
8							
9							
10							
11							
12							

DECISIONS

Week 29 beginning _____

AFFIRMATION

How gracious is Thy presence in the earth, O Lord. Be Thou the guide, that we with patience, may run the race which is set before us, looking to Thee, the Author, the Giver of Light.

262-24

PATIENCE

AWAKENERS

Each day before retiring, make a resume—not just mentally but upon paper—of what have been the *experiences* of the whole day. Make this not only a rule but a rule to do; not to be studied, not to be exploited or shown or given to others, but for self! And *do not* read same after it is written for at least thirty days. And then note the difference in what you are thinking and what you are thinking about, what your desires are, what your experiences are!

830-3

Take *time* to eat and to eat the right thing, giving time for digestive forces [to act] before becoming so mentally and bodily active as to upset digestion.

243-23

For, know—as He hath given—"Lo, I am with thee always, even unto the end." This is not a mere saying, but an awareness which one may find through that attuning through meditation, through prayer, through the opening of self for direction by Him.

69-4

BIBLE READING GUIDE

	OLD AND NEW TESTAMENTS	✔	NEW TESTAMENT ONLY
Sunday	Psalm 119		Acts 19:21-41
Monday	Psalms 120-131		Acts 20:1-16
Tuesday	Psalms 132-138		Acts 20:17-38
Wednesday	Psalms 139-143		Acts 21:1-17
Thursday	Psalms 144-150		Acts 21:18-40
Friday	Proverbs 1-3		Acts 22
Saturday	Proverbs 4-7		Acts 23:1-15

MY PRAYER LIST

MY DAILY DOZEN

DATE

	Sunday	Monday	Tuesday	Wednesday	Thursday	Friday	Saturday
1							
2							
3							
4							
5							
6							
7							
8							
9							
10							
11							
12							

DECISIONS

Week 30 beginning_____

AFFIRMATION

How gracious is Thy presence in the earth, O Lord. Be Thou the guide, that we with patience, may run the race which is set before us, looking to Thee, the Author, the Giver of Light.   262-24

PATIENCE

AWAKENERS

Then . . .make it a habit, make it a hobby, to at least each day, speak kindly to someone less fortunate than self. Not that there should be so much the contribution to organized charity, but have those charities of self [that] you never speak of, by speaking kindly to someone each day. This will let the body rest at night when it hasn't been able to, with its mental and material worries.   5177-2

In seeking, do not seek something afar, nor yet something new; rather that there are the proper ideals, the proper valuations of that *already* in hand. In using the opportunities in hand comes the understanding of larger, better, greater things; for whom the Lord loveth, to him is given *in hand* that which, if used, brings understanding and peace.   262-9

BIBLE READING GUIDE

	OLD AND NEW TESTAMENTS	✔	NEW TESTAMENT ONLY
Sunday	Proverbs 8-11		Acts 23:16-35
Monday	Proverbs 12-15		Acts 24
Tuesday	Proverbs 16-19		Acts 25
Wednesday	Proverbs 20-22		Acts 26
Thursday	Proverbs 23-26		Acts 27:1-26
Friday	Proverbs 27-31		Acts 27:27-44
Saturday	Ecclesiastes 1-4		Acts 28

MY PRAYER LIST

MY DAILY DOZEN

DATE

	Sunday	Monday	Tuesday	Wednesday	Thursday	Friday	Saturday
1							
2							
3							
4							
5							
6							
7							
8							
9							
10							
11							
12							

DECISIONS

Week 31 beginning_____

AFFIRMATION

How gracious is Thy presence in the earth, O Lord. Be Thou the guide, that we with patience, may run the race which is set before us, looking to Thee, the Author, the Giver of Light.   262-24

PATIENCE

AWAKENERS

. . .twice each day we would take grape juice (Welch's preferably); one ounce of the grape juice in half an ounce of water, half an hour before the meal—preferably the morning and the evening meals, especially.

With taking these, we find that the appetite will be more readily satisfied, and it will be a *reducing* nature of diet. . .   1657-2

Make *each* day as *some* activity that has brought joy, happiness, to someone else.   808-3

First study self, knowing first thy ideals spiritually, thy ideal mentally, thy ideal materially. Then study to show thyself [approved] unto that ideal, not passing quick judgment, not condemning anyone, but know what you believe and why. Most of all know the author of what you believe and as to whether it conforms to the ideal first spiritual, second mental, third in manifestation materially.   4035-1

BIBLE READING GUIDE

	OLD AND NEW TESTAMENTS	✔	NEW TESTAMENT ONLY
Sunday	Ecclesiastes 5-8		Romans 1
Monday	Ecclesiastes 9-12		Romans 2
Tuesday	Song of Solomon		Romans 3
Wednesday	Isaiah 1-4		Romans 4
Thursday	Isaiah 5-9		Romans 5
Friday	Isaiah 10-14		Romans 6
Saturday	Isaiah 15-21		Romans 7

MY PRAYER LIST

MY DAILY DOZEN

DATE

	Sunday	Monday	Tuesday	Wednesday	Thursday	Friday	Saturday
1							
2							
3							
4							
5							
6							
7							
8							
9							
10							
11							
12							

DECISIONS

Week 32 beginning _____

AFFIRMATION

How gracious is Thy presence in the earth, O Lord. Be Thou the guide, that we with patience, may run the race which is set before us, looking to Thee, the Author, the Giver of Light.   262-24

PATIENCE

AWAKENERS

A regular or well-balanced diet is well for this body. Keep plenty of foods that carry iodine, both as to vegetables and as to seafoods. These, the seafoods, we would have at least twice each week. This is best for this body as well as for most bodies.
                                                                         2981-2

Q. What studies would you recommend for my spiritual development?
A. First the New Testament, especially as related to John and Revelation. . .790-1

For, as has been given as one of the immutable laws, that which the mind of a soul—a SOUL—dwells upon it becomes; for mind is the builder. And if the mind is in attune with the law of the force that brought the soul into being, it becomes spiritualized in its activity. If the mind is dwelling upon or directed in that desire towards the activities of the carnal influences, then it becomes destructive in such a force.   262-63

BIBLE READING GUIDE

	OLD AND NEW TESTAMENTS	✔	NEW TESTAMENT ONLY
Sunday	Isaiah 22-26		Romans 8:1-21
Monday	Isaiah 27-31		Romans 8:22-39
Tuesday	Isaiah 32-37		Romans 9:1-15
Wednesday	Isaiah 38-42		Romans 9:16-33
Thursday	Isaiah 43-46		Romans 10
Friday	Isaiah 47-51		Romans 11:1-18
Saturday	Isaiah 52-57		Romans 11:19-36

MY PRAYER LIST

MY DAILY DOZEN

DATE

	Sunday	Monday	Tuesday	Wednesday	Thursday	Friday	Saturday
1							
2							
3							
4							
5							
6							
7							
8							
9							
10							
11							
12							

DECISIONS

Week 33 beginning

AFFIRMATION

As the Father knoweth me, so may I know the Father, through the Christ Spirit, the door to the kingdom of the Father. Show Thou me the way.   262-27

AWAKENERS

. . .occasionally—not too often—take the periods for the cleansing of the system with the use of the *apple diet;* that is:

At least for three days—two days or three days—take *nothing* except *apples—raw apples!* Of course, coffee may be taken if so desired, but no other foods but the raw apples. And then after the last meal of apples on the third day, or upon retiring on that evening following the last meal of apples, drink half a cup of olive oil.

This will tend to cleanse the system.   543-26

"What would Jesus have me do" regarding every question in thy relationships with thy fellow man, in thy home, in thy problems day by day. This rather should be the question, rather than "What shall I do?"   1326-1

BIBLE READING GUIDE

	OLD AND NEW TESTAMENTS	✔	NEW TESTAMENT ONLY
Sunday	Isaiah 58-63		Romans 12
Monday	Isaiah 64-66		Romans 13
Tuesday	Jeremiah 1-3		Romans 14
Wednesday	Jeremiah 4-6		Romans 15:1-13
Thursday	Jeremiah 7-10		Romans 15:14-33
Friday	Jeremiah 11-14		Romans 16
Saturday	Jeremiah 15-18		I Corinthians 1

MY PRAYER LIST

MY DAILY DOZEN

DATE

	Sunday	Monday	Tuesday	Wednesday	Thursday	Friday	Saturday
1							
2							
3							
4							
5							
6							
7							
8							
9							
10							
11							
12							

DECISIONS

Week 34 beginning _____

AFFIRMATION

As the Father knoweth me, so may I know the Father, through the Christ Spirit, the door to the kingdom of the Father. Show Thou me the way.   262-27

THE OPEN DOOR

AWAKENERS

. . .the active principles of Ipsab are constructive, especially, to the structural and circulatory activity of gums. For, as may be said of this compound, there are those principles and elements that are espcially adapted to the aiding of circulation and destruction of bacilli that forms or is an accumulation in the form of that which gathers on and in this portion of the body (the mouth, the gums and the teeth).

Hence, this is a universally beneficial property or compound for the teeth and gums. And the combination is such as to offer particular benefits for any condition where there is the tendency towards irritation in this portion of body.   275-31

Let age only ripen thee. For one is ever just as young as the heart and the purpose. Keep sweet. Keep friendly. Keep loving, if ye would keep young.   3420-1

BIBLE READING GUIDE

	OLD AND NEW TESTAMENTS	✔	NEW TESTAMENT ONLY
Sunday	Jeremiah 19-22		I Corinthians 2
Monday	Jeremiah 23-25		I Corinthians 3
Tuesday	Jeremiah 26-28		I Corinthians 4
Wednesday	Jeremiah 29-31		I Corinthians 5
Thursday	Jeremiah 32-33		I Corinthians 6
Friday	Jeremiah 34-36		I Corinthians 7:1-19
Saturday	Jeremiah 37-40		I Corinthians 7:20-40

MY PRAYER LIST

MY DAILY DOZEN

DATE

	Sunday	Monday	Tuesday	Wednesday	Thursday	Friday	Saturday
1							
2							
3							
4							
5							
6							
7							
8							
9							
10							
11							
12							

DECISIONS

Week 35 beginning _____

As the Father knoweth me, so may I know the Father, through the Christ Spirit, the door to the kingdom of the Father. Show Thou me the way.   262-27

THE OPEN DOOR

AWAKENERS

To make a success in *any* direction at the expense of body, mind, home, *or* relations with individuals, is to be lacking in that which may prevent the *real* self from entering into that of a contentment that must be the desire of *every* entity.   1925-2

Q. Would it be well to take a small quantity of olive oil daily?
A. Will be for most everyone. . ."   2072-16

. . .olive oil in small quantities. . .is rather beneficial, as it is a food for the intestinal system. . .   543-26

We know, and only need to be reminded, that the whole law is in Him. For, as He gave that which is the basis, the principle, of the intent and desire and purpose which should prompt our activity, so we in our own world—as we live, as we speak, as we pray—are to let it be in that tempo, in that way and manner which was prompted by Him, as He taught His disciples how to pray.   5749-12

BIBLE READING GUIDE

	OLD AND NEW TESTAMENTS	✔	NEW TESTAMENT ONLY
Sunday	Jeremiah 41-44		I Corinthians 8
Monday	Jeremiah 45-48		I Corinthians 9
Tuesday	Jeremiah 49-50		I Corinthians 10:1-18
Wednesday	Jeremiah 51-52		I Corinthians 10:19-33
Thursday	Lamentations 1-2		I Corinthians 11:1-16
Friday	Lamentations 3-5		I Corinthians 11:17-34
Saturday	Ezekiel 1-4		I Corinthians 12

MY PRAYER LIST

MY DAILY DOZEN

DATE

	Sunday	Monday	Tuesday	Wednesday	Thursday	Friday	Saturday
1							
2							
3							
4							
5							
6							
7							
8							
9							
10							
11							
12							

DECISIONS

Week 36 beginning_____

AFFIRMATION

As the Father knoweth me, so may I know the Father, through the Christ Spirit, the door to the kingdom of the Father. Show Thou me the way. 262-27

THE OPEN DOOR

AWAKENERS

In applying self, know thy own weaknesses, as well as thy own virtues. Set them down in a row, not in the same row; but every few weeks rub out those that you have overcome or add those that you know you have taken on. This will help you keep that balance that is so unusual in the entity.

Study spiritual things, mental things. For it is from these that the material things of life grow. 3652-1

Let the attitude then be *constructive* ever! See in the applications taken not just rote, not just something to be done, but—as the active force of every nature is God-influence working in and through the individual—see with each application the creating of energies necessary for bringing cooperation with the service the Creator would have thee render in thine experience. 1424-1

BIBLE READING GUIDE

	OLD AND NEW TESTAMENTS	NEW TESTAMENT ONLY
Sunday	Ezekiel 5-9	I Corinthians 13
Monday	Ezekiel 10-13	I Corinthians 14:1-20
Tuesday	Ezekiel 14-16	I Corinthians 14:21-40
Wednesday	Ezekiel 17-19	I Corinthians 15:1-28
Thursday	Ezekiel 20-21	I Corinthians 15:29-58
Friday	Ezekiel 22-24	I Corinthians 16
Saturday	Ezekiel 25-28	II Corinthians 1

MY PRAYER LIST

MY DAILY DOZEN

DATE

	Sunday	Monday	Tuesday	Wednesday	Thursday	Friday	Saturday
1							
2							
3							
4							
5							
6							
7							
8							
9							
10							
11							
12							

DECISIONS

Notes

Ideals Worksheet_____

   . . .the most important experience of this or any individual entity is to first know what *is* the ideal—spiritually.   357-13

SPIRITUAL	MENTAL	PHYSICAL

Week 37 beginning _____

AFFIRMATION

Our Father, who art in Heaven, may Thy kingdom come in earth through Thy presence in me, that the light of Thy word may shine unto those that I meet day by day. May Thy presence in my brother be such that I may glorify Thee. May I so conduct mine own life that others may know Thy presence abides with me, and thus glorify Thee. 262-30

IN HIS PRESENCE

AWAKENERS

Q. Suggest diet beneficial to preserving teeth.

A. Eggs, potato peelings, seafoods—all of these are particularly given to preserving the teeth; or anything that carries quantities of calcium or aids to the thyroids in its production would be beneficial—so it is not overbalanced, see?

Q. Is calcium taken in pills advisable?

A. That taken from vegetable matter is much more easily assimilated; or from fish *and* seafoods. 1523-3

Be not "sat upon" by disappointments. It is he who gets up each time that the Lord loves and will sustain. Know that the try is counted for righteousness and will bring *joy* into thy heart and into thy life. TRY! Pray often. *Try,* and walk often with Him—and He will walk and talk with thee. 3440-2

BIBLE READING GUIDE

	OLD AND NEW TESTAMENTS	✔	NEW TESTAMENT ONLY
Sunday	Ezekiel 29-32		II Corinthians 2
Monday	Ezekiel 33-36		II Corinthians 3
Tuesday	Ezekiel 37-39		II Corinthians 4
Wednesday	Ezekiel 40-42		II Corinthians 5
Thursday	Ezekiel 43-45		II Corinthians 6
Friday	Ezekiel 46-48		II Corinthians 7
Saturday	Daniel 1-3		II Corinthians 8

MY PRAYER LIST

MY DAILY DOZEN

DATE

	Sunday	Monday	Tuesday	Wednesday	Thursday	Friday	Saturday
1							
2							
3							
4							
5							
6							
7							
8							
9							
10							
11							
12							

DECISIONS

Week 38 beginning_____

AFFIRMATION

Our Father, who art in Heaven, may Thy kingdom come in earth through Thy presence in me, that the light of Thy word may shine unto those that I meet day by day. May Thy presence in my brother be such that I may glorify Thee. May I so conduct mine own life that others may know Thy presence abides with me, and thus glorify Thee.   262-30

IN HIS PRESENCE

AWAKENERS

At least make three people each day laugh heartily, by something the body says! It'll not only help the body; it'll help others!   798-1

Bolting food or swallowing it by the use of liquids produces more colds than *any one* activity of a diet! Even milk or water should be *chewed* two to three times before taken into the stomach. . .   808-3

Q. Can lost opportunities be redeemed?
A. Nothing is lost. Nothing is lost; we have used or abused our opportunities and there abide by them. In Him, through Him may they be blotted out, for "Though your sins be as scarlet, in Him they shall be as wool. He that heareth my voice and abideth in me shall *know* no lost opportunity!"   262-28

BIBLE READING GUIDE

	OLD AND NEW TESTAMENTS	✔	NEW TESTAMENT ONLY
Sunday	Daniel 4-6		II Corinthians 9
Monday	Daniel 7-9		II Corinthians 10
Tuesday	Daniel 10-12		II Corinthians 11:1-15
Wednesday	Hosea 1-6		II Corinthians 11:16-33
Thursday	Hosea 7-14		II Corinthians 12
Friday	Joel		II Corinthians 13
Saturday	Amos 1-5		Galatians 1

MY PRAYER LIST

MY DAILY DOZEN

DATE

	Sunday	Monday	Tuesday	Wednesday	Thursday	Friday	Saturday
1							
2							
3							
4							
5							
6							
7							
8							
9							
10							
11							
12							

DECISIONS

Week 39 beginning_____

AFFIRMATION

Our Father, who art in Heaven, may Thy kingdom come in earth through Thy presence in me, that the light of Thy word may shine unto those that I meet day by day. May Thy presence in my brother be such that I may glorify Thee. May I so conduct mine own life that others may know Thy presence abides with me, and thus glorify Thee.   262-30

IN HIS PRESENCE

AWAKENERS

Q. Spiritual foods?

A. These are needed by the body just as the body physical needs fuel in the diet. The body mental and spiritual needs spiritual food—prayer, meditation, thinking upon spiritual things. For thy body is indeed the temple of the living God. Treat it as such, physically and mentally.   4008-1

. . .olive oil. . .is one of the most effective agents for stimulating muscular activity, or mucous-membrane activity, that may be applied to the body.   440-3

In the application of the tenets, then, it is well to be sincere, but others may also be sincere. So, give each the same privilege of expression of his or her own opinions as demanded in self of others.

Tend to seek wherein ye do agree and not stress where you disagree. It will become apparent that indeed the Lord is one when it comes to glorifying His purpose in the earth.   3111-2

BIBLE READING GUIDE

	OLD AND NEW TESTAMENTS	✔	NEW TESTAMENT ONLY
Sunday	Amos 6 through Obadiah		Galatians 2
Monday	Jonah		Galatians 3
Tuesday	Micah		Galatians 4
Wednesday	Nahum through Habakkuk		Galatians 5
Thursday	Zephaniah through Haggai		Galatians 6
Friday	Zechariah 1-7		Ephesians 1
Saturday	Zechariah 8-14		Ephesians 2

MY PRAYER LIST

MY DAILY DOZEN

DATE

	Sunday	Monday	Tuesday	Wednesday	Thursday	Friday	Saturday
1							
2							
3							
4							
5							
6							
7							
8							
9							
10							
11							
12							

DECISIONS

Week 40 beginning_____

AFFIRMATION

Our Father, who art in Heaven, may Thy kingdom come in earth through Thy presence in me, that the light of Thy word may shine unto those that I meet day by day. May Thy presence in my brother be such that I may glorify Thee. May I so conduct mine own life that others may know Thy presence abides with me, and thus glorify Thee.   262-30

IN HIS PRESENCE

AWAKENERS

. . .never, under strain, when very tired, very excited, very mad, should the body take foods in the system, see? and never take any food that the body finds is not agreeing with same. . .   137-30

. . .the will of a soul, of a body, is supreme—even as to whether it makes of itself a channel for the spiritual influences in its experience or for the selfish desires of its own body and its aggrandizing of those influences.

Oh, if souls, bodies, everywhere, would gain that knowledge that the abilities to be sons of God or of the devil lie within self's own individual will! For, as has been given of old, "I am persuaded that neither personalities nor souls, individuals nor conditions, may separate me from the love of God save myself." To be that He would have thee be, in all that thou doest and hast done from day to day, is being then a channel—and being used by Him, rather than using the blessings He has given thee for thine own undoing.   416-2

BIBLE READING GUIDE

	OLD AND NEW TESTAMENTS	✔	NEW TESTAMENT ONLY
Sunday	Malachi		Ephesians 3
Monday	Matthew 1-4		Ephesians 4
Tuesday	Matthew 5-6		Ephesians 5:1-16
Wednesday	Matthew 7-9		Ephesians 5:17-33
Thursday	Matthew 10-11		Ephesians 6
Friday	Matthew 12		Philippians 1
Saturday	Matthew 13-14		Philippians 2

MY PRAYER LIST

MY DAILY DOZEN

DATE

	Sunday	Monday	Tuesday	Wednesday	Thursday	Friday	Saturday
1							
2							
3							
4							
5							
6							
7							
8							
9							
10							
11							
12							

DECISIONS

Week 41 beginning _____

AFFIRMATION

Our Father, our God, as we approach that that may give us a better insight of what He bore in the cross, what His glory may be in the crown, may Thy blessings—as promised *through Him*—be with us as we study together in His name.　　262-34

AWAKENERS

Q. Is there a meditation that can be used for building the body and keeping it in good condition? Please explain how this might be accomplished.

A. . . . a meditation, a centralizing, a localizing of the mind upon those portions of the system affected, or upon the activities needed for the physical being, *influences,* directs the principal forces of the system. And it does resuscitate, if kept in sincerity; not merely said as rote . . .

Lord, use Thou me—my body, my mind—in such a way and manner that I, as Thy servant, may fill those lives and hearts and minds I meet—day by day—with such hope and faith and power in Thy might, that it may bring the awareness of Thy presence into the experience of others as well as myself.　　1992-3

Stretch the body as a cat would stretch. This is the best exercise to keep body in proportion.　　5271-1

BIBLE READING GUIDE

	OLD AND NEW TESTAMENTS	✔	NEW TESTAMENT ONLY
Sunday	Matthew 15-17		Philippians 3
Monday	Matthew 18-20		Philippians 4
Tuesday	Matthew 21-22		Colossians 1
Wednesday	Matthew 23-24		Colossians 2
Thursday	Matthew 25-26		Colossians 3
Friday	Matthew 27-28		Colossians 4
Saturday	Mark 1-3		I Thessalonians 1

MY PRAYER LIST

MY DAILY DOZEN

DATE

	Sunday	Monday	Tuesday	Wednesday	Thursday	Friday	Saturday
1							
2							
3							
4							
5							
6							
7							
8							
9							
10							
11							
12							

DECISIONS

Week 42 beginning _____

AFFIRMATION

Our Father, our God, as we approach that that may give us a better insight of what He bore in the cross, what His glory may be in the crown, may Thy blessings—as promised *through Him*—be with us as we study together in His name.   262-34

THE CROSS AND THE CROWN

AWAKENERS

For the hydrotherapy and massage are preventive as well as curative measures. For the cleansing of the system allows the body-forces themselves to function normally, and thus eliminate poisons, congestions and conditions that would become acute throughout the body.   257-254

Q. What exercises are best for me?
A. Walking is the best exercise of all. Any outdoor life or activity is well, if taken regularly; but to take such activity spasmodically is not well for any—nor for this body.
      2477-1

. . .knowing that the promise of the Christ is, "Lo, I am with thee always, even unto the end of the world."
He was in the beginning, He is the end. And as ye walk in the light of His promise, of His words, ye may know the way ye go. For His light shineth in the darkness and maketh the paths straight for those that seek His face.   2454-4

BIBLE READING GUIDE

	OLD AND NEW TESTAMENTS	✔	NEW TESTAMENT ONLY
Sunday	Mark 4-5		I Thessalonians 2
Monday	Mark 6-7		I Thessalonians 3
Tuesday	Mark 8-9		I Thessalonians 4
Wednesday	Mark 10-11		I Thessalonians 5
Thursday	Mark 12-13		II Thessalonians 1
Friday	Mark 14-16		II Thessalonians 2
Saturday	Luke 1		II Thessalonians 3

MY PRAYER LIST

MY DAILY DOZEN

DATE

	Sunday	Monday	Tuesday	Wednesday	Thursday	Friday	Saturday
1							
2							
3							
4							
5							
6							
7							
8							
9							
10							
11							
12							

DECISIONS

Week 43 beginning —————

AFFIRMATION

Our Father, our God, as we approach that that may give us a better insight of what He bore in the cross, what His glory may be in the crown, may Thy blessings—as promised *through Him*—be with us as we study together in His name.   262-34

THE CROSS AND THE CROWN

AWAKENERS

Yet if the body becomes so health-conscious or so addicted to routines for this or that, it will be just as serious as if the body did little or nothing about it except try to carry on with its work.   4374-1

Coffee prepared properly is a food (that is, without cream or milk). Coffee old or stale, or overdone, is bad for *any*body!   271-4

When caffeine is allowed to remain in the colon, there is thrown off from same poisons. Eliminated. . .coffee is a food value and is preferable to many stimulants that might be taken. . .   294-86

Know deep within self that God hath need of thee at this time. Know that He came into the world that each individual, each entity, might have life more abundantly; that is, more of life, more expectancy from life, and more worthwhile experiences. 3671-1

BIBLE READING GUIDE

	OLD AND NEW TESTAMENTS	✔	NEW TESTAMENT ONLY
Sunday	Luke 2-3		I Timothy 1
Monday	Luke 4-5		I Timothy 2
Tuesday	Luke 6-7		I Timothy 3
Wednesday	Luke 8-9		I Timothy 4
Thursday	Luke 10-11		I Timothy 5
Friday	Luke 12-13		I Timothy 6
Saturday	Luke 14-16		II Timothy 1

MY PRAYER LIST

MY DAILY DOZEN

DATE

	Sunday	Monday	Tuesday	Wednesday	Thursday	Friday	Saturday
1							
2							
3							
4							
5							
6							
7							
8							
9							
10							
11							
12							

DECISIONS

Week 44 beginning_____

AFFIRMATION

Our Father, our God, as we approach that that may give us a better insight of what He bore in the cross, what His glory may be in the crown, may Thy blessings—as promised *through Him*—be with us as we study together in His name.   262-34

AWAKENERS

If there is the application of self to spiritual purposes, mental ideals, the result will be a balanced physical, mental and spiritual body. But the spiritual purposes must be centered in Creative Forces and not in the self or in that way of selfishness. 4084-1

Plenty of lettuce should always be eaten by most *every* body; for this supplies an effluvium in the bloodstream itself that is a destructive force to *most* of those influences that attack the bloodstream. It's a purifier.   404-6

Know that thy body, thy mind, thy soul, is a manifestation of God in the earth—as is every other soul; and that thy body is indeed the temple of the living God. All the good, then, all the God, then, that ye may know, is manifested in and through thyself. . .
2970-1

BIBLE READING GUIDE

	OLD AND NEW TESTAMENTS	✔	NEW TESTAMENT ONLY
Sunday	Luke 17-18		II Timothy 2
Monday	Luke 19-20		II Timothy 3
Tuesday	Luke 21-22		II Timothy 4
Wednesday	Luke 23-24		Titus 1
Thursday	John 1-3		Titus 2
Friday	John 4-5		Titus 3
Saturday	John 6-8		Philemon

MY PRAYER LIST

MY DAILY DOZEN

DATE

	Sunday	Monday	Tuesday	Wednesday	Thursday	Friday	Saturday
1							
2							
3							
4							
5							
6							
7							
8							
9							
10							
11							
12							

DECISIONS

Order my next Day by Day book from A.R.E. (order form on page 144)

Week 45 beginning____

AFFIRMATION

As my body, mind and soul are one, Thou, O Lord, in the manifestations in the earth, in power, in might, in glory, art one. May I see in that I do, day by day, more of that realization, and manifest the more.   262-38

THE LORD THY GOD IS ONE

AWAKENERS

There must be a certain amount of recreation. There must be certain amounts of rest. These are physical, mental and spiritual necessities. Didn't God make man to sleep at least a third of his life?   3352-1

. . .do not combine also the reacting acid fruits with starches, other than *whole wheat bread!* that is, citrus fruits, oranges, apples, grapefruit, limes or lemons or even tomato juices. And do not have cereals (which contain the greater quantity of starch than most) at the same meal with the citrus fruits.   416-9

. . .there is a whole day's work before thee each day, with all its glorious opportunities of seeing the glory of the Lord manifested by thine own acts!. . .Study, then, to show thyself approved, *each day! Do what* thou *knowest* to do, to be aright! Then *leave it alone!* God giveth the *increase!*   601-11

BIBLE READING GUIDE

	OLD AND NEW TESTAMENTS	✔	NEW TESTAMENT ONLY
Sunday	John 9-10		Hebrews 1
Monday	John 11-12		Hebrews 2
Tuesday	John 13-16		Hebrews 3
Wednesday	John 17-18		Hebrews 4
Thursday	John 19-21		Hebrews 5
Friday	Acts 1-3		Hebrews 6
Saturday	Acts 4-6		Hebrews 7

MY PRAYER LIST

MY DAILY DOZEN

DATE

	Sunday	Monday	Tuesday	Wednesday	Thursday	Friday	Saturday
1							
2							
3							
4							
5							
6							
7							
8							
9							
10							
11							
12							

DECISIONS

Week 46 beginning___

AFFIRMATION

As my body, mind and soul are one, Thou, O Lord, in the manifestations in the earth, in power, in might, in glory, art one. May I see in that I do, day by day, more of that realization, and manifest the more.   262-38

THE LORD THY GOD IS ONE

AWAKENERS

For, He has not willed that any soul perish. Thus continuously, today, now, He presents ever a way in which each soul may find its relationships to Creative Forces and thus fulfill the purpose for which it entered this present material experience.
1688-6

Worry and fear being, then, the greatest foes to *normal* healthy physical body, turning the assimilated forces in the system into poisons that must be eliminated, rather than into life-giving vital forces for a physical body.   5497-1

For, to each entity, each soul, there is ever the ministering angel before the throne of grace, the throne of God. The ministering angel is the purposefulness, the spirit with which ye would do anything in relationship to others.   3357-2

BIBLE READING GUIDE

	OLD AND NEW TESTAMENTS	✔	NEW TESTAMENT ONLY
Sunday	Acts 7-8		Hebrews 8
Monday	Acts 9-10		Hebrews 9
Tuesday	Acts 11-13		Hebrews 10:1-18
Wednesday	Acts 14-16		Hebrews 10:19-39
Thursday	Acts 17-19		Hebrews 11:1-19
Friday	Acts 20-22		Hebrews 11:20-40
Saturday	Acts 23-25		Hebrews 12

MY PRAYER LIST

MY DAILY DOZEN   **DATE**

	Sunday	Monday	Tuesday	Wednesday	Thursday	Friday	Saturday
1							
2							
3							
4							
5							
6							
7							
8							
9							
10							
11							
12							

DECISIONS

Week 47 beginning _____

AFFIRMATION

As my body, mind and soul are one, Thou, O Lord, in the manifestations in the earth, in power, in might, in glory, art one. May I see in that I do, day by day, more of that realization, and manifest the more.   262-38

THE LORD THY GOD IS ONE

AWAKENERS

Find self. For, as is indeed understood, and may be gained more and more, purposes, desires, aims, hopes, while they may be only mental, if they are entertained within the bodily experience they become realities—by their application in one's relationships to others.   2082-1

Do be mindful of the diet. Include in the diet often raw vegetables prepared in various ways, not merely as a salad but scraped or grated and combined with gelatin . . .
3445-1

. . . He has given in the earth that which, when sought by the individual entity or soul that acknowledges it has gone astray, helps to meet whatever condition that may have come to pass. For, as given, "Though ye wander far, if ye call I will hear, and answer speedily."
And this may be *you,* if you will but harken.   3124-1

BIBLE READING GUIDE

	OLD AND NEW TESTAMENTS	✔	NEW TESTAMENT ONLY
Sunday	Acts 26-28		Hebrews 13
Monday	Romans 1-3		James 1
Tuesday	Romans 4-7		James 2
Wednesday	Romans 8-10		James 3
Thursday	Romans 11-13		James 4
Friday	Romans 14-16		James 5
Saturday	I Corinthians 1-4		I Peter 1

MY PRAYER LIST

MY DAILY DOZEN   **DATE**

	Sunday	Monday	Tuesday	Wednesday	Thursday	Friday	Saturday
1							
2							
3							
4							
5							
6							
7							
8							
9							
10							
11							
12							

DECISIONS

Week 48 beginning _____

AFFIRMATION

As my body, mind and soul are one, Thou, O Lord, in the manifestations in the earth, in power, in might, in glory, art one. May I see in that I do, day by day, more of that realization, and manifest the more.   262-38

THE LORD THY GOD IS ONE

AWAKENERS

Be *glad* you have the opportunity to be alive at this time, and to be a part of that preparation for the coming influences of a spiritual nature that *must* rule the world...Be happy of it, and give thanks daily for it.   2376-3

...as is known to the body—all work and no play will eventually wear the physical, or so warp the *mental* into those channels that the best may *not* be given, either in the mental way or in the physical, and the application of same then comes to naught.
5616-1

Let the light of His countenance rest upon thee and bring thee peace. Let His ways be thy ways. Let joy and happiness be ever in thy word, in thy song. Let *hopefulness*, helpfulness, ever be thy guide. The Lord is thy shepherd; let Him keep thy ways.
938-1

BIBLE READING GUIDE

	OLD AND NEW TESTAMENTS	✔	NEW TESTAMENT ONLY
Sunday	I Corinthians 5-9		I Peter 2
Monday	I Corinthians 10-13		I Peter 3
Tuesday	I Corinthians 14-16		I Peter 4
Wednesday	II Corinthians 1-4		I Peter 5
Thursday	II Corinthians 5-8		II Peter 1
Friday	II Corinthians 9-13		II Peter 2
Saturday	Galatians 1-3		II Peter 3

MY PRAYER LIST

MY DAILY DOZEN

DATE

	Sunday	Monday	Tuesday	Wednesday	Thursday	Friday	Saturday
1							
2							
3							
4							
5							
6							
7							
8							
9							
10							
11							
12							

DECISIONS

Notes

Ideals Worksheet_____

   . . .the most important experience of this or any individual entity is to first know what *is* the ideal—spiritually.   357-13

SPIRITUAL	MENTAL	PHYSICAL

Week 49 beginning_____

AFFIRMATION

Our Father, through the love that Thou has manifested in the world through Thy Son, the Christ, make us more aware of GOD IS LOVE.   262-43

LOVE

AWAKENERS

All [vitamins] that add to the system are more efficacious if they are given for periods, left off for periods and begun again. For if the system comes to rely upon such influences wholly, it ceases to produce the vitamins even though the food values may be kept normally balanced.

And it's much better that these be produced in the body from the normal development than supplied mechanically; for nature is much better *yet* than science!

This as we find, then, given. . .left off. . .and then begun again, especially through the winter months, would be much more effective with the body.   759-12

For all prayer is answered. Don't tell God how to answer it. Make thy wants known to Him. Live as if ye expected them to be answered. For He has given, "What ye ask in my name, believing, that will my Father in heaven give to thee." Again it has been said, and truly, the Father will not withhold any good thing from those who love His coming.
     4028-1

BIBLE READING GUIDE

	OLD AND NEW TESTAMENTS	✔	NEW TESTAMENT ONLY
Sunday	Galatians 4-6		I John 1
Monday	Ephesians 1-3		I John 2
Tuesday	Ephesians 4-6		I John 3
Wednesday	Philippians		I John 4
Thursday	Colossians		I John 5
Friday	I Thessalonians		II John
Saturday	II Thessalonians		III John

MY PRAYER LIST

MY DAILY DOZEN

DATE

	Sunday	Monday	Tuesday	Wednesday	Thursday	Friday	Saturday
1							
2							
3							
4							
5							
6							
7							
8							
9							
10							
11							
12							

DECISIONS

Week 50 beginning_____

AFFIRMATION

Our Father, through the love that Thou has manifested in the world through Thy Son, the Christ, make us more aware of GOD IS LOVE.   262-43

LOVE

AWAKENERS

Q. What causes colds? Can you give me a formula or method of preventing them or curing them?
A. Keep the body alkaline! Cold germs do not live in an alkaline system! They do breed in any acid or excess of acids of *any* character left in the system.   1947-4

Q. What foods are acid-forming for this body?
A. All of those that are combining fats with sugars. Starches naturally are inclined for acid reaction. But a normal diet is about twenty percent acid to eighty percent alkaline-producing.   1523-3

Take time first to be holy. Don't let a day go by without meditation and prayer for some definite purpose and not for self, but that self may be the channel of help to someone else. For in helping others is the greater way to help self.   3624-1

BIBLE READING GUIDE

	OLD AND NEW TESTAMENTS	✔	NEW TESTAMENT ONLY
Sunday	I Timothy		Jude
Monday	II Timothy		Revelation 1
Tuesday	Titus through Philemon		Revelation 2-3
Wednesday	Hebrews 1-4		Revelation 4
Thursday	Hebrews 5-7		Revelation 5
Friday	Hebrews 8-10		Revelation 6
Saturday	Hebrews 11-13		Revelation 7

MY PRAYER LIST

MY DAILY DOZEN   **DATE**

	Sunday	Monday	Tuesday	Wednesday	Thursday	Friday	Saturday
1							
2							
3							
4							
5							
6							
7							
8							
9							
10							
11							
12							

DECISIONS

Week 51 beginning_____

AFFIRMATION

Our Father, through the love that Thou has manifested in the world through Thy Son, the Christ, make us more aware of GOD IS LOVE. 262-43

LOVE

AWAKENERS

A body is more susceptible to cold with an excess of acidity *or* alkalinity, but *more* susceptible in case of excess acidity. For, an alkalizing effect is destructive to the cold germ.

When there has been at any time an extra depletion of the vital energies of the body, it produces the tendency for an excess acidity—and it may be throughout any portion of the body.

At such period, if a body comes in contact with one sneezing or suffering with cold, it is more easily contracted.

Thus precautions are to be taken at such periods especially. 902-1

". . .He that gives a cup of water in *His* name loses not *his* reward"—not as pay, not as recompense, but *service* is asked of all men, rather than sacrifice. In sacrifice there is penance, but grace doth more greatly abound to him who sheds the love of the Father upon those that the body may contact from day to day. 99-8

BIBLE READING GUIDE

	OLD AND NEW TESTAMENTS	✔	NEW TESTAMENT ONLY
Sunday	James		Revelation 8-9
Monday	I Peter 1-2		Revelation 9-10
Tuesday	I Peter 3-5		Revelation 11
Wednesday	II Peter		Revelation 12
Thursday	I John 1-3		Revelation 13
Friday	I John 4-5		Revelation 14
Saturday	II John, III John, Jude		Revelation 15

MY PRAYER LIST

MY DAILY DOZEN

DATE

	Sunday	Monday	Tuesday	Wednesday	Thursday	Friday	Saturday
1							
2							
3							
4							
5							
6							
7							
8							
9							
10							
11							
12							

DECISIONS

Week 52 beginning _____

AFFIRMATION

Our Father, through the love that Thou has manifested in the world through Thy Son, the Christ, make us more aware of GOD IS LOVE.   262-43

LOVE

AWAKENERS

There might have been many changes—there might have been defiances in the past that would have brought changes. But look not back upon what might have been. Rather, as given, lift up, look up—now—where ye are.   369-16

Avoid too much of the heavy meats [pork, beef] not well cooked. Eat plenty of vegetables of all characters. The meats taken would be preferably fish, fowl and lamb; others *not* so often. Breakfast bacon, crisp, may be taken occasionally. These as we find are the better foods. . .   1710-4

Be not afraid because ye have faltered anywhere. For He has said, "I forgive, even as ye forgive others."
Then how forgiving art thou? Answer this, and ye will know just how ye have been forgiven. It is the law, it is the Lord, it is love.   3376-2

BIBLE READING GUIDE

	OLD AND NEW TESTAMENTS		NEW TESTAMENT ONLY
Sunday	Revelation 1-3		Revelation 16
Monday	Revelation 4-6		Revelation 17
Tuesday	Revelation 7-9		Revelation 18
Wednesday	Revelation 10-12		Revelation 19
Thursday	Revelation 13-15		Revelation 20
Friday	Revelation 16-18		Revelation 21
Saturday	Revelation 19-22		Revelation 22

MY PRAYER LIST

MY DAILY DOZEN

DATE

	Sunday	Monday	Tuesday	Wednesday	Thursday	Friday	Saturday
1							
2							
3							
4							
5							
6							
7							
8							
9							
10							
11							
12							

DECISIONS

Meditation _____

We may define meditation as attuning the physical body and the mental body to the spiritual by practicing the silence. Meditation is reestablishing our at-onement with God and meeting Him within the temple of our own body.

THE PURPOSE OF MEDITATION

The purpose of meditation should never be "for" but "to." We do not meditate *for* something just as we do not love someone *for* something. The true spirit of meditation is more to express love than to receive recompense. It is true that highly desirable consequences follow the regular practice of meditation; but if we have set out to achieve these things as *goals* of meditation, we have defeated ourselves from the outset. It is the *spirit* in which we approach the Divine within that is the key factor in meditation.

Meditation helps us to fulfill the great commandment to love God with all our heart and mind and soul. In any love affair, we want to be near the loved one. "To love God with all our hearts" should be accompanied by a desire to be near and one with Him. We practice a period of silence in order to express our love for God. Psychic development, better health, uplift of spirit, and other benefits will result from meditation; but the ultimate fruit of the spirit is love. Thus love is the purpose—as well as the outcome—of meditation.

PREPARATION FOR MEDITATION

There are several methods of preparation which may be considered. The following are offered as suggestions or guidelines. If we are seeking growth in attunement, then preparation for meditation must be a continuing activity. We should begin some kind of physical exercise. We should eat those things we know will help attune the physical body. We must feed ourselves a mental diet of positive thinking. Meditation does not stand alone. It exists within the context of our intentions to do something constructive about the overall pattern of our lives.

Specifically, in our preparation for each meditation session, the readings recommend a prayer of protection just preceding the quiet time. One such prayer is: "Father, as I open myself to the unseen forces surrounding the throne of grace and beauty and might, I throw about myself the protection found in the thought of the Christ."

THE PRACTICE OF MEDITATION

There are some proper techniques which should be followed. The spine should be straight to facilitate the flow of the life force through the seven spiritual centers. The mind must be centered with a singleness of eye to focus the flow of the life force. The spirit must be quickened through desire with a high sense of purpose. Silence and stillness must be maintained. However, many times we expect these techniques to guarantee results whether or not the heart and mind and soul are centered devotedly on Him.

If the purpose of life is to become more loving, as we have been commanded, then the practice should relate to that purpose. If God is a loving spirit, we can attune to Him only by awakening a loving spirit within ourselves. We do not attune to the Spirit by virtue of technique but rather *in response to our own seeking spirit, the quality of our desire to love Him.*

As we turn within, we are likely to discover what we hold as obstacles between ourselves and our awareness of oneness with God. When we try to be quiet, even for just a minute, we may observe where our consciousness goes. *That* is what we are centered upon, rather than God. What we think and worry about is what we hold in our minds and hearts in preference to an awareness of His Spirit. As soon as we become aware of our wandering thoughts, we need to acknowledge that these things separate us from Him, affirm that only with His help will things turn out right. Or, in the case of pleasant thoughts, thank Him and then return heart, mind and soul to loving Him.

We should never evaluate the effectiveness of our meditation by the experiences we have in those minutes of silence. Meditation is not seeking "a high" in that period. It is rather practicing a regular invitation—day in, day out, week after week, month after month—an invitation for the Spirit of God to flow through us, to transform us and to enable us to live more effectively and in a more loving way.

How to Obtain
Guidance on Decisions_____

One of the most exciting and promising of all of the statements in the readings is the assurance that there is no question we can ask that cannot be answered from within. The readings gave very specific and detailed information to many individuals on how to go about decision making with confidence and assurance.

"Q. How can one be sure that a decision is in accordance with God's will?

"A. As indicated here before. Ask self in the own conscious self, 'Shall I do this or not?' The voice will answer within. Then meditate, ask the same, Yes or No. You may be very sure if thine own conscious self and the divine self are in accord, you are truly in that activity indicated, 'My spirit beareth witness with thy spirit.' You can't get far wrong in following the word, as ye call the word of God." 2072-14

From the point of view of the readings, there is *no* question, however seemingly inconsequential or highly significant, which should not be approached in this way. The steps are:

1. Set the ideal.

2. Pose the question so that it may be answered "yes" or "no." If we are willing to work through the process of posing the question so that it may indeed by answered by "yes" or "no," we may clarify not only the question but also the answer. The greater the clarity in the question, the less ambiguous may be the answer.

3. Decide. A choice must be made. At this point, we may bring to bear all of our reasoning, logic, good judgment and the implications of the facts as we understand them. Now we are to make our best logical decision.

4. Measure the decision by the ideal. Does the decision we made measure up to our ideal in such circumstances? Sometimes the right decision may be made for the wrong reasons! In the course of our decision-making process, we may receive a "no" to a decision because of the *motive* on which it was based rather than the desirability of the outcome.

5. Meditate. This meditation is not upon the question but rather it is a period of *quiet* for the purpose of attunement. At the end of the attunement period, the question may be reintroduced in a prayerful spirit, as in "Lord, I have decided to do this yet Thou knowest best. Be Thou the guide. Yes or No?" Then,

6. Listen! We do not specifically listen for "a voice" although that may indeed occur. We may have a visual experience, we may receive an affirmation or a proverb related to the decision, we may simply have a sense of rightness or a sense of being ill at ease about the decision we have made. An answer usually just "comes."

If we find one voice saying "yes" and another saying "no," back and forth in an indecisive manner, we need not force the decision at that time. As we place it in the hands of God, we may later receive a more clear sense of direction through a dream, a new insight or a new perspective. We must be cautious at this point about trying to read external signs instead of listening to the voice within. After all, the whole purpose of this approach is based on the assurance that we meet God within and that we can grow in our ability to sense His inner direction.

7. Measure the decision again by the ideal. Once a sense of guidance is gained from the inner attunement (especially if the decision is changed), it must again be measured by the ideal. We are seeking a final decision which is consistent with our highest ideal and this depends on how well we make an inner attunement.

8. Do it! The readings warn that we must not make decisions in this manner and then fail to act on them.

9. Be thankful. The marvelous promise of a life guided by His Spirit should be valued, cherished and appreciated in the deepest sense.

It is recommended that this procedure be used repeatedly on low-effort, low-cost, low-risk decisions so that we may learn clearly how the procedure works for us personally. This is a life process—not a single event. As we begin to make decisions in this manner and act upon them, we begin to grow in confidence, understanding the many factors involved in the procedure.

We should not stop seeking help on a decision with just one attempt. The success of Step 6 depends, of course, on the measure of attunement we attain in Step 5. At one time we may be less centered or less attuned than at another time. If a decision is correct, we should get the same answer several times. God will not be unhappy with our willingness to double- or triple-check.

Suggestions for Daily Dozen Activities —————

In applying self, then, know. . .that as ye use that thou hast in hand day by day the next step may be given thee. Not all at once, for these become rather overpowering if more is gained than may be used in the present.   1695-1

Meditation
A morning walk
Add gelatin to salads
Read the Bible
Eliminate fried foods
Eat three almonds
Raw vegetable salad
Dark bread instead of white
Use Ipsab
Reduce coffee or tea intake
Eat breakfast
7½ to 8 hours sleep
Evening exercises
Pray for those on prayer list
Make 3 people laugh
Eliminate carbonated drinks
Smile at a stranger
Be optimistic
Colonic or enema
Peanut oil massage
Spinal adjustment
Apple diet

Glass of water upon arising
Glass of water mid-morning
Glass of water mid-afternoon
Glass of water before meals
6 to 8 glasses of water daily
Head & neck exercise—morning
Head & neck exercise—evening
An evening walk
Record dreams
Eliminate milk/cream from coffee
Apply Study Group discipline
20% acid/80% alkaline diet
Stretching exercises—morning
Complain about nothing
Reading to improve mental diet
Do breathing exercise
Eat more leafy vegetables
Bless food before eating
Castor oil pack
Study A Search for God chapter
Outreach to a friend
Practice eating slowly

Exercises _____

HEAD AND NECK
And take the head and neck exercise regularly; this for the head, the neck, the eyes, and the organs of the sensory system.   3008-1

Sitting erect bend the head forward three times at least, then back as far as it may be bent three times; to the right side three times; then to the left side three times. Then circle the head and neck to the right three times, then to the left three times. Be consistent with this though, not just doing it occasionally.   5404-1

**At least two
times per day**

BREATHING, STRETCHING AND BENDING
Three to five minutes of morning and evening—before an open window, of course—that of rising on the toes with the hands gradually raised above the head at the same time, breathing in deeply. The better way is to breathe first through one nostril, then the other, but this is not easily done—in the beginning. This is the best exercise that may be taken by most any body...Two to three times through each nostril is the better way, for the expansion of the lungs and for the purifying of circulation by same. Breath *in* through the nostril, *out* through the mouth—when taking such exercise.   2533-3

Of morning, and upon arising especially (and don't sleep too late!)—and before dressing, so that the clothing is loose or the fewer the better—standing erect before an open window, breathe deeply; gradually raising hands *above* the head, and then with the circular motion of the body from the hips bend forward; breathing *in* (and through the nostrils) as the body rises on the toes—breathing very deep; *exhaling suddenly* through the *mouth; not* through the nasal passages. Take these for five to six minutes. Then as these progress, gradually *close* one of the nostrils (even if it's necessary to use the hand—but if it is closed with the left hand, raise the right hand; and

137

when closing the right nostril with the right hand, then raise the left hand) *as* the breathing *in* is accomplished. Rise, and the circular motion of the body from the hips, and bending forward; *expelling* as the body reaches the lowest level in the bending towards the floor (expelling through the mouth, suddenly). 1523-2

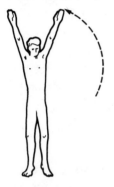 

**Mornings for
five or six minutes**

HIP CIRCLES

. . .a regular exercise would be helpful, but don't start this and then do it for a day and then skip two or three days and then try it again; either do it regularly or don't begin; an exercise the body may take itself. This take for about two minutes morning and evening; evening after it has prepared for retiring. On the floor with the hands, the feet to the wall, raise and then lower body three or four times; then a circular motion of the body on the hands, see? This isn't easy, but it will strengthen the whole condition of the spine, keep the abdominal muscles well as to general position of the body and keep the limbs in shape as to strengthen the muscles without being detrimental to any portion of the body. This will help the circulation, aid the digestion and improve the general conditions of the body. This do at least three times; that is, raise and lower the body three times and circle the body at least three times, morning and evening. 308-13

Circular motion

**Raise and lower
three or four times**   **to the right
three times**   **to the left
three times**

STRETCHING AND LIMBERING EXERCISES

For maintaining flexibility and muscle tone, begin doing the following exercises gradually, building over time to series of a half dozen to a dozen.

Shoulder circles for deltoids. Begin with hands describing small circles and gradually increase the diameter of the circles as your muscles warm up. Repeat, circling arms in the opposite direction.

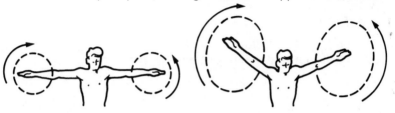

Side exercises for external obliques and lower back

Half-squats for thighs and respiratory and circulatory systems

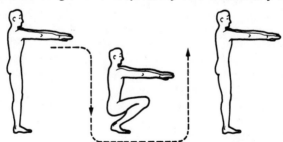

ABDOMINAL SERIES

Isometric

**One-half sit up twist
with knee pulled up**

**Scissors (legs 6″ off floor;
cross right foot under, left foot over; then reverse)**

Diet Review Sheet

DIRECTIONS

Circle 1: 80%* of your daily food intake should consist of foods from this circle.

Circle 2: 20% of your daily food intake should consist of foods from this circle.

Circle 3: Include these foods about three times a week.

Circle 4: Avoid these foods.

*80% means four out of five average helpings of food should come from the center circle.

MENU SAMPLE

BREAKFAST
Citrus fruit or cereal. (Do not combine these at the same meal.)
Boiled or scrambled egg
Whole wheat toast
Glass of milk

LUNCH
Have a completely RAW lunch and/or vegetable soup
Include green leafy vegetables in a combination salad with oil dressing or mayonnaise
One slice bread and butter
Beverage

SUPPER
Meat: Fish, fowl or lamb
Cooked vegetables
Include a variety of above and below ground, yellow and green vegetables
Dessert if desired
Beverage

Courtesy of the A.R.E. Clinic, Inc., Phoenix, Arizona

Affirmations from
A Search for God, Book II ————————

OPPORTUNITY

In seeking to magnify Thy name, Thy glory, through that Thou dost make manifest in me, O Lord, be Thou the guide, and—day by day, as the opportunity is given—let my hands, my mind, my body, do that Thou wouldst have me do as Thine own in the earth; for, as I manifest, may Thy glory become known to those through the love, the promises Thou hast made in Thy Son.   262-49

DAY AND NIGHT

In Thy mercies, O heavenly Father, wilt Thou be the guide in the study of the manifestations of Thy love, even as in "Day unto day uttereth speech and night unto night sheweth knowledge." So may the activities of my life, as a representative of Thy love, be a manifestation in the earth.   262-54

GOD THE FATHER AND HIS MANIFESTATIONS

May the desire of my heart be such that I become more and more aware of the spirit of the Father, through the Christ, manifesting in me.   262-57

DESIRE

Father, let Thy desires be my desires. Let my desires, God, be Thy desires, in spirit and in truth.   262-60

DESTINY OF THE MIND

Lord, Thou art my dwelling place! In Thee, O Father, do I trust! Let me see in myself, in my brother, that Thou would bless in Thy Son, Thy gift to me that I might know Thy ways! Thou hast promised, O Father, to hear when Thy children call! Harken, that I may be kept in the way that I may know the glory of Thy Son as Thou hast promised in Him, that we through Him might have access to Thee! Thou, O God, alone, can save! Thou alone can keep my ways!   262-73

DESTINY OF THE BODY

Lord, use me in *whatever* way or manner that *my* body may be as a living example of Thy love to the brethern of our Lord.   262-84

DESTINY OF THE SOUL
Lord, let me—my mind, my body, my soul—be at one with Thee: That I—through Thy promises in Him, Thy Son—may know Thee more and more. 262-88

GLORY
Open Thou mine eyes, O God, that I may know the glory Thou hast prepared for me. 262-89

KNOWLEDGE
Let the knowledge of the Lord so permeate my being that there is less and less of self, more and more of God, in my dealings with my fellow man; that the Christ may be in all, through all, in His name.

262-95

WISDOM
Our Father, our God, may the light of Thy wisdom, of Thy strength, of Thy power, guide—as we would apply ourselves in Thy service for others. In His name we seek. 262-102

HAPPINESS
Our Father, our God, in my own consciousness let me find happiness in the love of Thee, for the love I bear toward my fellow man. Let my life, my words, my deeds, bring the joy and happiness of the Lord in Jesus to each I meet day by day. 262-106

SPIRIT
Father, God, in Thy mercy, in Thy love, be Thou with us now. For we know and we speak of Thy love.

And help us then to put away, for the hour, the cares of this life; that we may know in truth that the Spirit and the Lamb say, "Come."

Let they that hear also say, "Come."

Let all that will, come and drink of the water of life. 262-113

THE WORK OF EDGAR CAYCE TODAY

The Association for Research and Enlightenment, Inc. (A.R.E.®), is a membership organization founded by Edgar Cayce in 1931.

- 14,256 Cayce readings, the largest body of documented psychic information anywhere in the world, are housed in the A.R.E. Library/Conference Center in Virginia Beach, Virginia. These readings have been indexed under 10,000 different topics and are open to the public.

- An attractive package of membership benefits is available for modest yearly dues. Benefits include: a journal and newsletter; lessons for home study; a lending library through the mail, which offers collections of the actual readings as well as one of the world's best parapsychological book collections, names of doctors or health care professionals in your area.

- As an organization on the leading edge in exciting new fields, A.R.E. presents a selection of publications and seminars by prominent authorities in the fields covered, exploring such areas as parapsychology, dreams, meditation, world religions, holistic health, reincarnation and life after death, and personal growth.

- The unique path to personal growth outlined in the Cayce readings is developed through a worldwide program of study groups. These informal groups meet weekly in private homes.

- A.R.E. maintains a visitors' center where a bookstore, exhibits, classes, a movie, and audiovisual presentations introduce inquirers to concepts from the Cayce readings.

- A.R.E. conducts research into the helpfulness of both the medical and non-medical readings, often giving members the opportunity to participate in the studies.

A.R.E., Dept. C., P.O. Box 595
Virginia Beach, VA 23451, (804) 428-3588

———————————ORDER FORM———————————

A.R.E.® Press, P.O. Box 595, Virginia Beach, VA 23451

Please send me _____ copy(ies) of *Day by Day* (311P) at $5.95 ea. $_____

Virginia Residents add 4% tax   _____

Post. & Handling Each Destination: Inside U.S.A. $.95   _____

Outside U.S.A. $3.00   _____

Total Enclosed   _____

Non-U.S. residents must make payments in United States funds. Sorry, no C.O.D. Prices subject to change without notice.

Please Indicate Method of Payment:

☐ Check or Money Order payable to A.R.E. Press   ☐ Master Card   ☐ VISA

Card No. [ ][ ][ ][ ][ ][ ][ ][ ][ ][ ][ ][ ][ ][ ][ ][ ] Exp. Date | MO. | YR. |

Signature _____

Your Name _____

Address _____

City _____

State _____ Zip _____